DATE DUE

The Future of Renewable Energy

What Is the Future of Biofuels?

Carla Mooney

ReferencePoint Press®

San Diego, CA

About the Author

Carla Mooney is the author of many books for young adults and children. She lives in Pittsburgh, Pennsylvania, with her husband and three children.

For more information, contact:
ReferencePoint Press, Inc.
PO Box 27779
San Diego, CA 92198
www. ReferencePointPress.com

Picture Credits:
Cover: Thinkstock.com
Steve Zmina: 17, 22, 31, 36, 43, 48, 55, 63
Thinkstock/photos.com: 9

LIBRARY OF CONGRESS CATALOGING-IN-PUBLICATION DATA

Mooney, Carla, 1970-
What is the future of biofuels? / by Carla Mooney.
   p. cm. -- (Future of renewable energy series)
Includes bibliographical references and index.
ISBN-13: 978-1-60152-272-6 (hardback : alk. paper)
ISBN-10: 1-60152-272-X (hardback : alk. paper)
1. Biomass energy--Juvenile literature. I. Title.
TP339.M66 2013
662'.88--dc23
                                                        2012011484

Contents

Foreword

What are the long-term prospects for renewable energy?

In his 2011 State of the Union address, President Barack Obama set an ambitious goal for the United States: to generate 80 percent of its electricity from clean energy sources, including renewables such as wind, solar, biomass, and hydropower, by 2035. The president reaffirmed this goal in the March 2011 White House report *Blueprint for a Secure Energy Future*. The report emphasizes the president's view that continued advances in renewable energy are an essential piece of America's energy future. "Beyond our efforts to reduce our dependence on oil," the report states, "we must focus on expanding cleaner sources of electricity, including renewables like wind and solar, as well as clean coal, natural gas, and nuclear power—keeping America on the cutting edge of clean energy technology so that we can build a 21st century clean energy economy and win the future."

Obama's vision of America's energy future is not shared by all. Benjamin Zycher, a visiting scholar at the American Enterprise Institute, a conservative think tank, contends that policies aimed at shifting from conventional to renewable energy sources demonstrate a "disconnect between the rhetoric and the reality." In *Renewable Electricity Generation: Economic Analysis and Outlook* Zycher writes that renewables have inherent limitations that can be overcome only at a very high cost. He states: "Renewable electricity has only a small share of the market, and ongoing developments in the market for competitive fuels . . . make it likely that renewable electricity will continue to face severe constraints in terms of competitiveness for many years to come."

Is Obama's goal of 80 percent clean electricity by 2035 realistic? Expert opinions can be found on both sides of this question and on all of the other issues relating to the debate about what lies ahead for renewable energy. Driven by this reality, *The Future of Renewable Energy* series critically examines the long-term prospects for renewable energy by delving into the topics and opinions that dominate and inform renewable energy policy and debate. The series covers renewables such as solar, wind, biofuels, hydrogen, and hydropower and explores the issues of cost and affordability, impact on the environment, viability as a replacement for fossil fuels, and what role—if any—government should play in renewable energy development. Pointed questions (such as "Can Solar Power Ever Replace Fossil Fuels?" or "Should Government Play a Role in Developing Biofuels?") frame the discussion and support inquiry-based learning. The pro/con format of the series encourages critical analysis of the topics and opinions that shape the debate. Discussion in each book is supported by current and relevant facts and illustrations, quotes from experts, and real-world examples and anecdotes. Additionally, all titles include a list of useful facts, organizations to contact for further information, and other helpful sources for further reading and research.

Visions of the Future: Biofuels

Four decades ago Brazil imported more than 80 percent of its fuel, mainly oil, from other countries. Today Brazil is an energy-independent country. It reached that milestone in large part because of biofuels.

Brazil is the world's second largest producer of the biofuel ethanol; only the United States produces more. South America's largest country relies on sugarcane to make biofuels. In 2010 Brazil used more than half of its sugarcane crop to produce approximately 6.9 billion gallons (26.1 billion L) of ethanol.

Most of Brazil's ethanol powers cars. In 2003 Brazil introduced flexible-fuel vehicles (FFVs), which have engines that run on ethanol, gasoline, or a mixture. Today 80 percent of Brazil's cars have flexible-fuel engines. The FFV's success has led Brazil to explore ways to use ethanol fuel for motorcycles, buses, and airplanes.

Ethanol production is being applied to more than vehicles, however. At many Brazilian ethanol-processing plants, sugarcane waste is being used to produce heat and power. Excess power is sometimes sold to local governments. In the city of Piracicaba, a processing plant burns the sugarcane plant's woody residue to supply about half the city's electricity needs. In 2010 the state-run oil company Petrobras announced that it had designed the world's first ethanol-fueled power plant. "We have great expectations to show the viability and economy of generating electricity from . . . an alternative feedstock to fossil fuels,"[1] says Maria das Gracas Foster, head of Petrobras's natural gas division.

A Model for the Future

Today Brazil is considered the world's biofuel leader and a model for the future as other countries seek to reduce reliance on fossil fuels and become energy independent. By producing biofuel energy rather than relying on other countries, Brazil avoids price swings that are commonplace in the world energy market. This saves Brazil billions of dollars in energy costs.

Brazil also sells ethanol to other countries. According to the Brazilian Sugarcane Industry Association, Brazil exported 2.75 billion liters (0.73 billion gallons) of ethanol for the 2009–2010 crop year. "We are moving fast to the wholesale export of ethanol. . . . We're investing in infrastructure in Brazil to make it easier to export in large quantities,"[2] says Jose Gabrielli, chief executive of Petrobras, which oversees ethanol sales abroad. The exports could grow larger if Brazil expands its sugarcane fields onto 148 million acres (60 million ha) of available lands. In that scenario, scientists estimate Brazil's biofuel could supply 14 percent of the world's fuel, making Brazil the world's dominant sugarcane ethanol supplier.

A Worldwide Source of Energy

The fossil fuels oil, coal, and natural gas currently provide most of the world's energy for electricity and transportation. Fossil fuel supply, however, is limited and nonrenewable. Most experts agree that as fossil fuel supplies dwindle, the world will need alternative energy sources. In addition, the burning of fossil fuels releases into the air pollutants that have been linked to acid rain, greenhouse gases, and negative impacts on human health. Fossil fuel concerns have led to an increased focus on alternative energy sources. Of the alternative fuels, biofuel is one of the most widely used and considered among the best options for meeting the world's future energy needs.

Biofuels are liquid and gaseous fuels produced from biomass—organic material from plants or animals. Biomass energy can be made from sources such as wood waste, corn kernels, agricultural or forest residues, food waste, and other industrial waste materials. Power plants can burn biomass plant material to produce heat or electricity. Biomass can be chemically fermented to make liquid fuel such as ethanol or pressed for oil to make biodiesel. In addition, it can be digested by bacteria to create methane gas that powers turbines. It can also be heated under special conditions to create a gas that can be burned for electricity or used in many products.

First-Generation Biofuels

Biofuels are generally divided into two main categories. Conventional, or first-generation, biofuels are well established and produced on a commercial scale. Conventional biofuels include sugar- and starch-based ethanol, oil-crop-based biodiesel, and vegetable oil. Feedstocks used for conventional biofuels include sugarcane, corn, wheat, rapeseed, soybean, and oil palm. First-generation biofuels are made from proven technology, such as burning or chemical fermentation.

Worldwide, ethanol is the most common first-generation biofuel. Ethanol is primarily used as a transportation fuel and blended with gasoline. According to the US Department of Energy (DOE), the United States is the world's largest ethanol producer, generating 13 billion gallons (49.2 billion L) in 2010. Ethanol can be produced from different feedstocks, including sugarcane and corn. In the United States, ethanol-gasoline blends are typically 10 percent ethanol. The biofuel industry expects the level of ethanol in such blends to increase to 85 percent or more in the future.

Biodiesel, more common in Europe than in the United States, is another biofuel. It is created from vegetable or microalgae oil. Most biodiesel is used in compression-ignition, or diesel, engines and blended with petroleum diesel.

Advanced Biofuels

Many scientists believe that first-generation biofuels are a bridging technology until the next generation of advanced biofuels is ready for commercial use. Instead of using food crops, researchers are developing

Sugarcane (pictured) has made Brazil the world's biofuel leader. It is a model for the future as other countries seek to reduce reliance on fossil fuels and become energy independent.

advanced biofuels from new feedstocks. Many are concentrating on cellulose, found in nonfood grasses and woody plants such as switchgrass and willow. Other researchers are investigating algae's potential to produce biofuel. "As world population grows and energy demands increase, these products and technologies will play an important role in meeting that demand,"[3] says Alan Shaw, CEO of Codexis, an industrial biotechnology company.

Advanced biofuels promise to be more efficient than first-generation technologies. Advanced biofuels use more of the plant itself, such as corn crop residue that is left behind during corn ethanol production, to produce fuel. Cellulosic sources also require less energy to grow than food crops, and once the cellulosic conversion process is ready for commercial use, part of the biomass can be used to power the production process.

Although promising, the technology to create advanced biofuels is still under development. Breaking down cellulose is more difficult and expensive than creating biofuel from corn or sugarcane. To date, no commercial-scale cellulosic or algae biofuels plants are operating in the United States, mainly because of cost.

Advantages of Biofuels

Biofuels are a promising energy source. They are renewable, clean, and reduce dependence on imported oil. Unlike fossil fuels, which are found primarily in the Middle East (oil and natural gas), North America (coal), and Russia (coal), biofuels are made from renewable resources that can be found worldwide. According to the DOE, "Biomass is a clean, renewable energy source that can help to significantly diversify transportation fuels in the United States."[4]

Biofuels are also environmentally friendly. Biofuels contain no sulfur and have low toxic emissions. In addition, using biofuels instead of fossil fuels can reduce greenhouse gas emissions. According to the Argonne National Laboratory, corn-based ethanol production and use can reduce greenhouse gas emissions by 52 percent. Biofuels made from sugarcane ethanol and cellulosic sources are projected to reduce greenhouse gas emissions even more.

Biofuels can also reduce dependence on imported oil. Currently, the United States imports more than half of its oil from foreign countries. This puts the country at risk for political, military, or economic conflicts. According to the DOE, "Biofuels must continue to play a significant role as we work aggressively to diversify our nation's energy sources and provide a balanced portfolio of energy solutions to help meet our growing demand for energy."[5]

Challenges Ahead

Despite its potential, biofuel faces several challenges. Current world biofuel production relies on food crops, primarily corn, soybeans, and wheat. As food crops have been diverted into energy production, food prices have risen and shortages have occurred. According to Lester Brown of the Earth Policy Institute, "We used to have a food economy and an energy economy. The two are merging. We need to . . . think through carefully what we're doing."[6]

Although promising, advanced biofuels are years away from commercial-scale production. Whether new technologies and feedstocks can produce efficient and affordable biofuels on a commercial scale remains to be seen. "I haven't seen anyone really do a fair calculation of what algae can do, and until I see that, I'm not convinced,"[7] says Jay Keasling, a biofuel researcher at the University of California at Berkeley.

In addition, significant investment in biofuel distribution networks is needed before widespread use can occur. Currently, no pipelines to pump biofuel from processing plants to users exist. Instead, biofuel distribution relies on more expensive and less efficient rail and truck transportation.

Once biofuel reaches gas stations, their owners will need to build new pumps and stations to sell higher-blend biofuel. Currently, only a fraction of US gas stations sell higher-blend ethanol fuel. In addition, consumers will need to purchase new cars to use the fuel. Currently, only about 3 percent of US cars are FFVs that can use higher-blend ethanol fuel.

An Important Future

Despite the challenges, research that will establish biofuels as an integral part of the world's renewable energy future is ongoing. As world energy demands increase, fossil fuel alternatives must be developed. For biofuels, the future may rest on the industry's ability to develop technology to harvest energy economically from advanced biofuel sources. "While the research into advanced biofuels continues and innovations are taking place, significant challenges must be overcome to ensure they can become economic and affordable at large scale,"[8] says John McDonald, Chevron Corporation chief technology officer.

Chapter One

Are Biofuels Affordable?

Biofuels Are Affordable

Biofuels are an affordable alternative fuel now and will be even more afford-able in the future as technology improves, as more feedstocks become avail-able, and as production increases. The cost benefits of biofuels, however, have broader financial implications. Because biofuels can be produced domesti-cally rather than purchased abroad, the US economy will benefit through job creation and money spent at home. And because biofuels emit fewer pollut-ants and greenhouse gases than fossil fuels, costs to human health and the environment will be significantly lower—another factor that enhances the affordability of biofuels.

The Debate

Biofuels Are Too Costly

Biofuels are too costly and inefficient to be a viable source of transportation fuel and electricity. Ethanol biofuel costs more per gallon than traditional gasoline. In addition, current production, transportation, and delivery systems for ethanol fuel are limited. Widespread use of biofuel will require significant up-front expen-ditures to build new plants, pipelines, and fueling stations, and consumers will incur added costs to purchase more expensive FFVs. Also, the use of food crops to produce biofuel has been linked to increasing world food prices and shortages. This makes biofuel even more costly for society.

Biofuels Are Affordable

"Ethanol is the most affordable and clean-burning alternative to gasoline."

—Brian Jennings, executive vice president of the American Coalition for Ethanol.

Brian Jennings, "Ethanol: Affordable, Clean and We Don't Have to Wait," *Hill*, May 11, 2010. www.thehill.com.

The biofuel industry is young, but as it develops, biofuels promise to be an affordable alternative fuel. Innovations in various areas have already improved the efficiency of turning corn and sugarcane into ethanol. Innovations in farming, for example, have significantly decreased the amount of energy needed to produce ethanol, as have more efficient fertilizer and pesticide use, higher-yielding crops, and more energy-efficient conversion technology.

According to a May 2010 report from the University of Illinois at Chicago, the energy needed to produce ethanol has decreased 28 percent since 2001. At the same time, ethanol yields have increased by 5.3 percent, allowing the same amount of corn to be converted into more energy. As researchers develop new technologies, especially those that turn nonfood sources such as woody biomass and algae into fuel, biofuel costs will fall even further. As these technologies mature, biofuel's price will become even more competitive with gasoline and diesel fuel. "Within 5 to 10 years at least half a dozen [biofuel] technologies will be competitive even with $60 per barrel oil,"[9] says Vinod Khosla, a venture capitalist specializing in clean energy technology.

Conversion Technology Improves

Biofuel production costs generally depend on several factors, including conversion technology complexity, feedstock costs, and scale of the processing plant. Conversion, or the process of turning biomass feedstock into fuel, is one of the most expensive steps in making biofuels. To reduce costs, researchers are working on more efficient conversion technologies.

In 2011 the DOE announced a $30 million project aimed at accomplishing this goal. Plants Engineered to Replace Oil (PETRO) is tasked with developing crops that capture more energy from the sun and convert that energy directly into fuels. The project will fund technologies that deliver more energy per acre with less processing. One PETRO project is at the University of Florida, where researchers are working to increase the production of turpentine, a natural liquid biofuel, from pine trees. Researchers estimate that fuel produced from these trees could become a sustainable domestic biofuel. They predict production of approximately 100 million gallons (378.5 million L) of fuel annually from less than 25,000 acres (10,117 ha) of forestland. In a 2011 press release announcing the project, the DOE states, "If successful, PETRO will create biofuels from domestic sources such as tobacco and pine trees for half their current cost, making them cost-competitive with fuels from oil."[10]

> "Within 5 to 10 years at least half a dozen [biofuel] technologies will be competitive even with $60 per barrel oil."[9]
>
> —Vinod Khosla, a venture capitalist specializing in clean energy technology.

Advanced Biofuel Feedstocks Will Cost Less

Feedstock costs are another critical component of making biofuels affordable. According to the International Energy Agency (IEA), feedstock accounts for 45 to 70 percent of total production costs for conventional biofuels. Advanced biofuels use cheaper feedstocks, which account for only 25 to 40 percent of total production cost. As a result, experts predict that overall biofuel feedstock costs will drop as energy crops, waste, and residues become the predominant source of biomass. "Regardless of the technology, feedstock costs will be critical. For instance, I believe prices for woody biomass and agricultural waste . . . will drop within a decade,"[11] says Khosla.

Advanced biofuels will also become cheaper as transportation costs decrease. Currently, harvesting and transporting advanced biomass such as forest and farm residue is expensive because it is bulky, difficult to handle, and spread across a wide geographic area. Scientists are developing preprocessing technologies such as grinding piles of biomass so that it can be more easily transported to biorefineries. To reduce the cost of collecting forest and farm waste that is located over large geographical areas, the industry is designing new, lighter containers and trucks that will reduce truck traffic and transportation costs. These improvements will decrease biomass supply costs, driving down biofuel's cost. Among industry leaders participating in a 2011 roundtable discussion was Guido Ghisolfi, CEO of Beta Renewables Italy. Ghisolfi predicts that advanced biofuels will become cost-competitive in the energy market. "For the first time we will not only see advanced biofuels competitive with first generation fuels," Ghisolfi says, "but the challenge will be brought to fossil fuels."[12]

Reducing Capital Costs

Biofuel costs will also drop as production plants increase their scale and production efficiencies. When biofuel is produced in larger volumes, fixed costs are spread across more gallons of fuel, making each less expensive. A 2011 cost analysis by the International Energy Agency predicts that advanced biofuel's cost will be equivalent to the cost of petroleum gasoline by about 2030. "Within the industry, we are addressing the challenge of developing cost effective means of converting non-food energy sources, or biomass, into fermentable sugars and ultimately to alternative forms of energy and sustainable products,"[13] says Alan Shaw.

To increase biofuel production, new processing plants and infrastructure must be built. Initially, short-term capital costs will be incurred to build new plants and infrastructure. Yet as plants scale up to commercial size, particularly for advanced biofuels, the fuel's cost per gallon will come down.

One way some companies are trying to reduce capital and production costs is by colocating, or adding biofuel processing to an existing power plant, instead of building a new plant. The company also saves money by sharing expenses with the power plant. "Co-location brings considerable value to the cellulosic ethanol plant as well, through both direct cost savings and operation efficiency. In addition to lower capital and equipment costs, the expenses for labor, warehousing, site development, and energy can also be reduced,"[14] says Frances Williams, a specialist with biofuel company Novozymes.

Society Reaps Economic Benefits

The biofuel industry's growth will provide economic benefits by adding jobs and money to local communities where they are produced. According to an analysis by renewable fuel economist John Urbanchuk, the US production and use of 13 billion gallons (49.2 billion L) of ethanol fuel in 2010 supported more than 400,000 American jobs. These jobs included positions for ethanol production, delivery, services, and suppliers. In addition, according to a 2011 Renewable Fuels Association report, the ethanol industry added $36 billion in wages to US household income in 2010 and $53.6 billion to the gross domestic product, a measure of US economic activity.

Cellulosic biofuels can also provide farmers with a new income source. Currently, farms generate a significant amount of agricultural waste with a high cellulosic content. Waste such as corn fiber, corn leaves and stalks, sugar cane fiber, rice hulls, and wheat straw can be sold to cellulosic biofuel-processing plants, creating a major new market for farmers. The incentive to profit from farm waste will push farmers to innovate farming practices to get more from their land and develop new ways to provide cellulose along with traditional crops. According to the Natural Resources Defense Council, "If farmers can sell different parts of the same plant to different markets, they can increase their revenues and diversify their risk,"[15] In this way, biofuels will bring economic benefits to the farming community.

Advances in conversion technology have cut the amount of energy needed to convert feedstock into biofuel, and this trend is expected to continue in the future. According to the Renewable Fuels Association, the average ethanol plant used 28 percent less thermal energy per gallon in 2008 than in 2001. As a result of these advances, the cost of making ethanol is also becoming much less expensive.

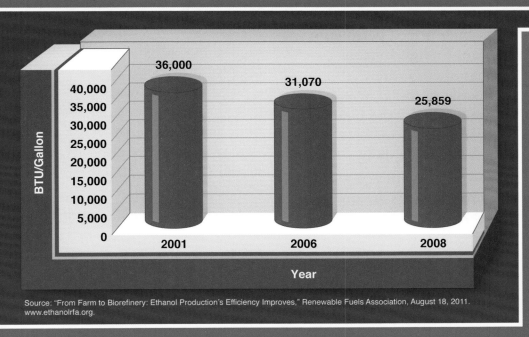

Energy Use per Gallon of Ethanol Produced

Source: "From Farm to Biorefinery: Ethanol Production's Efficiency Improves," Renewable Fuels Association, August 18, 2011. www.ethanolrfa.org.

Biofuels Reduce Hidden Costs

Not only do biofuels bring economic benefits to the community, they also reduce environmental, health care, and security costs associated with fossil fuels. Burning fossil fuels releases pollutants into the air that have been linked to acid rain, greenhouse gases, and negative impacts on human health. As a result, society incurs significant environmental cleanup and health care costs. According to a 2009 report by the National Academy of Sciences, burning fossil fuels, primarily oil and coal, costs the United States about $120 billion annually in health care costs. Using biofuels instead of fossil fuels reduces emissions and greenhouse gases in the atmosphere. According to the DOE, using biofuels can reduce greenhouse gases by as much as 85 percent, depending on the type of feedstock and processing used. Reducing these pollutants will decrease the costs of environmental cleanup and pollution-related health care.

Along with the economic benefits of reduced environmental costs, domestic biofuel production can reduce costs the United States incurs to protect its foreign oil interests. These costs can be extremely volatile due to political instability around the world. Prior to the 2001 Iraq War, the National Defense Council Foundation (NDCF) estimated that the fixed costs of defending Middle East oil were approximately $50 billion annually. In a follow-up study, the NDCF estimated that oil defense costs soared to $137.8 billion in 2006. In contrast, biofuels made from locally sourced materials eliminate the need for these expenditures. "Shouldn't the cost of the U.S. forces keeping the oil and gas flowing from the Middle East be added to the cost of oil?"[16] asks Wesley K. Clark, retired US Army general. If so, Clark says, the cost of biofuel would be recognized as a true bargain compared with oil.

> "I would tell someone who knows very little about our industry that we [ethanol producers] are an essential answer to high priced petroleum from foreign sources that are too often hostile to the U.S. We are better for the U.S. economy, better for the environment, better for the rural economy, and when all costs are on the table, the lowest cost for the consumer."[17]
>
> —Mick Henderson, general manager of Commonwealth AgriEnergy, a corn ethanol producer.

An Affordable Choice

When evaluating the affordability of biofuels, the broad range of costs incurred by fossil fuels versus the broad range of cost benefits of biofuels is important to consider. Technology advances are steadily lowering the cost of biofuel feedstocks and production, and this will undoubtedly continue well into the future. In addition, using biofuel has many other economic and social benefits, making it an attractive and affordable energy choice. "I would tell someone who knows very little about our industry that we [ethanol producers] are an essential answer to high priced petroleum from foreign sources that are too often hostile to the U.S. We are better for the U.S. economy, better for the environment, better for the rural economy, and when all costs are on the table, the lowest cost for the consumer,"[17] says Mick Henderson, general manager of Commonwealth AgriEnergy, a corn ethanol producer.

Biofuels Are Too Costly

> "There's no evidence that biofuels are going to be cost effective anytime soon."

—Dan Simmons, director of state and regulatory affairs at the Institute for Energy Research, a free-market energy think tank.

Quoted in Fred Lucas, "Navy Biofuel Deal Is 'Cost Prohibitive,' 'Another Solyndra,' Critics Say," CNSNews.com, December 23, 2011. http://cnsnews.com.

Biofuels are too costly and inefficient to compete with fossil fuels and other alternative energy sources—both now and in the future. At current oil prices, ethanol costs more per gallon than traditional gasoline. According to a July 2011 DOE report, the average price of regular gasoline is $3.68 per gallon (per 3.8 L). In comparison, high-blend ethanol and biodiesel cost $4.60 and $4.13 per gallon, respectively.

Higher cost at the pump is not the only downside to the affordability of biofuels. High-blend biofuel can only be used in more expensive FFVs. In every way, biofuel is too costly to be a realistic fuel option for the average consumer. "Biofuels must also be affordable for consumers. . . . Biofuels that cost more than traditional fuels will provide no incentive to potential consumers [to buy them],"[18] says John McDonald.

Not only do biofuels cost more per gallon, they also have lower fuel efficiency than gasoline. A gallon (3.8 L) of ethanol provides a vehicle with only two-thirds of the energy in a gallon of gasoline. As a result, consumers using ethanol fuels need to purchase larger quantities to run their vehicles for the same distances. A 2011 test by *Consumer Reports* found that highway fuel economy dropped by nearly 30 percent when using an 85 percent ethanol blend as compared with straight gasoline. "The biggest problem [with corn ethanol] is just the straight-out economics and the costs. The energy input/output is not very good,"[19] says Stephen Polasky, a professor of ecological and environmental economics at the University of Minnesota.

Expensive Distribution Systems Needed

Large-scale use of biofuels, especially corn-based ethanol, is hindered by a limited and expensive transportation and distribution network. Most US ethanol plants are concentrated in the Midwest, where corn grows. Gasoline consumption, however, is greatest along the East and West Coasts. To date, dedicated pipelines such as those that pump gasoline out of oil wells and refineries near the Gulf of Mexico do not exist for ethanol. Ethanol would not be able to share the oil pipeline network because ethanol is water soluble and will mix easily with any water present in a pipeline. Water does not affect oil during distribution, but ethanol that absorbs too much water during transport becomes unsuitable for use. Instead, more expensive trains and trucks carry 90 percent of ethanol across the country, and this is unlikely to change anytime soon.

Even if ethanol could be widely and inexpensively distributed, a ready supply of vehicles to use it does not exist. Although most cars can use lower ethanol-gasoline blends, only about 3 percent of the nation's vehicles are capable of running on mid-level or higher blends. High-blend ethanol can damage the engine of a conventional car. For that car to run on high-blend ethanol without damage, expensive changes would be needed in the car's fuel system, including its fuel injectors, and in its computer system. Plastic and aluminum materials would need to be designed to avoid damage when exposed to ethanol.

> "Biofuels must also be affordable for consumers. . . . Biofuels that cost more than traditional fuels will provide no incentive to potential consumers [to buy them]."[18]
>
> —John McDonald, Chevron Corporation vice president and chief technology officer.

Furthermore, even if more FFVs were on the road, finding a fueling station would be a challenge. According to the Renewable Fuels Association, fuel-dispensing infrastructure limits the sale of ethanol biofuel. To distribute the higher ethanol blends, new fuel pumps must be installed or existing fuel pumps must be fitted with new technology. Out of the approximately 160,000 gas stations in the United States, only 2,600 offer designated biofuel pumps. An additional 900 stations have pumps

21

Ethanol Costs More than Gasoline at the Pump

Biofuel is not an affordable alternative to gasoline. Over the past 10 years, the most common ethanol fuel (an 85 percent blend called E85) has consistently cost more per gallon than gasoline and is expected to remain more expensive in the future.

US Average Gasoline and E85 Retail Prices

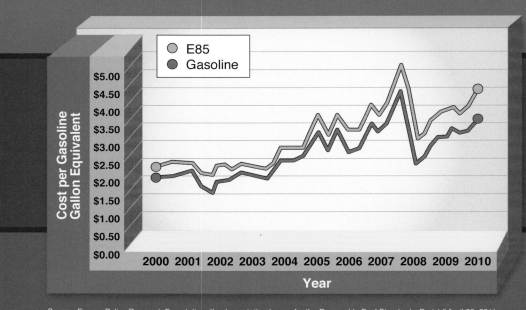

Source: Energy Policy Research Foundation, "Implementation Issues for the Renewable Fuel Standard—Part 1," April 28, 2011. www.eenews.net.

that can blend higher levels of ethanol with gasoline. To handle higher ethanol blends, gas stations would also have to invest in new—or convert existing—storage tanks, systems, and equipment. According to estimates from the DOE website, installing a single higher-blend ethanol system can cost thousands of dollars. When multiplied across the country, this adds up to millions of dollars in up-front capital investment.

Food Versus Fuel

Production and distribution are not the only factors that drive up the cost of biofuels and make them an unaffordable source of fuel and energy for the future. In the United States in particular, but also in other biofuel-producing countries, biofuels are made primarily from food crops. Diverting crops for fuel is reducing the world's food supply and, as a result, driving food prices higher. Cassava, a starchy root that is a major staple food in Africa and Asia is being used to make biofuel in China. Rapeseed, one of the world's sources of vegetable oil, is being made into biodiesel in Europe. Moreover, sugar cane and corn are being turned into ethanol in several countries. In 2011 the United Nations Food and Agriculture Organization reported that the global food price index had peaked at its highest point in 20 years. "Biofuels are contributing to higher prices and tighter markets,"[20] says Timothy Searchinger, a research scholar at Princeton University.

In the United States nearly 40 percent of the corn crop is used for making fuel. In the second half of 2010, the price of corn rose 73 percent. The United Nations World Food Program says this happened in part because more US corn is being used to produce biofuels. "Ethanol uses 4.9 billion bushels of corn in the U.S.," says Lester Brown. "That's enough grain to feed 350 million people."[21]

Food experts say that corn price increases in America have a ripple effect around the world. "How much does the price of corn in Chicago influence the price of corn in Rwanda? It turns out there is a correlation," says Marie Brill, senior policy analyst at ActionAid, an international development group. Following the rise of corn prices in the United States, the price of corn in Rwanda rose 19 percent in 2010. "For Americans it may mean a few extra cents for a box of cereal," she says. "But that kind of increase puts corn out of the range of impoverished people."[22]

In addition to rising grain prices, the use of crops for fuel may also cause the price of meat and vegetables to rise. Biofuel sources like cassava chips are commonly used as animal feed in Asia. As the biofuel industry increases cassava demand, cassava prices increase. Meat producers who pay higher cassava prices to feed their animals will pass on the additional cost to consumers in the form of higher meat prices. In other places, farmers may choose to grow biofuel crops that earn more money than growing vegetables or rice. These changes would reduce food supply and increase prices.

Almost 60 percent of the world's population is malnourished. In some poor countries like Bangladesh, rising food prices have sparked riots and political unrest. As a result, some people are calling on countries to slow their rush into biofuel production and preserve an adequate supply of crops for human consumption. "It's pretty simple—corn that could go for food or fuel is diverted to fuel," says Brill. "That influences prices."[23]

Costly Technology Might Not Work

Producing advanced biofuels at an affordable, commercial scale has proved to be more difficult than expected. The cellulose in many advanced biofuel feedstocks is more difficult to break down into the sugars needed to make biofuel than the starch in corn or sugarcane. Currently, several technologies can break down cellulose. It can be heated at high pressure with oxygen to form synthesis gas that can be turned into ethanol and other fuels. Industrial enzymes can break down cellulose into sugars, which ferment in reactors with microorganisms to make ethanol. However, to date these processes are too expensive for commercial use, and they are unlikely to become less expensive anytime in the near future.

> "The scale-up of advanced biofuels is highly capital-intensive; a full-scale plant can cost well over $100 million."[24]
>
> —Pavel Molchanov, analyst at Raymond James, a financial services company that researches the energy market.

In addition, production facilities for advanced biofuel require significant upfront capital expenditures. Experts estimate that production facilities for cellulosic biofuel are currently 10 to 15 times more expensive than a traditional oil refinery. "The scale-up of advanced biofuels is highly capital-intensive; a full-scale plant can cost well over $100 million,"[24] says analyst Pavel Molchanov of Raymond James, a financial services company that researches the energy market.

In addition, the current technology to convert biomass into fuel cannot produce the necessary volumes. The Energy Independence and Security Act of 2007 calls for 16 billion gallons (60.6 billion L) of advanced cellulosic biofuels to be blended into transportation fuels by 2022. Currently, the United States produces well under 1 million gallons (3.8 million L) of advanced cellulosic biofuel annually. According to the US Department of Agriculture, the biofuel industry would need to invest approximately $168 billion to build more than 500 new advanced biofuel production facilities just to meet the 2022 target. "It's going to take substantial innovation and technology breakthroughs to grow, harvest, gather, transport, and transform extensive volumes of biomass into a . . . liquid fuel that is economic and affordable at such scale,"[25] says McDonald.

Biofuels are too costly and inefficient to compete effectively with other energy sources. The technology to produce biofuels at a reasonable price and in sufficient quantities simply does not yet exist, and this will apparently not change in the near future.

Chapter Two

How Do Biofuels Impact the Environment?

Biofuels Are Environmentally Friendly

Biofuels are an environmentally friendly, renewable source of energy. Biofuel use releases fewer greenhouse gases into the atmosphere and, as a result, helps reduce global warming. In addition, biofuels emit fewer pollutants, improving air quality. On land, planting some biofuel feedstocks can slow soil erosion, keep pollutants from entering waterways, and provide a natural habitat for many species. In addition, biofuels are biodegradable and break down into compounds that are not toxic to the environment if spilled or leaked.

The Debate

Biofuels Harm the Environment

The environmental benefits of biofuels have been overstated. In some cases biofuels can even harm the environment. In theory, generating energy from plants is appealing; plants absorb carbon dioxide from the air as they grow and then release that carbon dioxide when burned as fuel, resulting in a near zero net carbon emission. In reality, biofuel production is more complicated than that. Biofuel production harms the environment by increasing emissions of greenhouse gases, polluting land and water, consuming valuable land and water resources, and damaging biodiversity around the world.

Biofuels Are Environmentally Friendly

"There is no fuel available at scale today that can match ethanol's ability to improve overall environmental quality compared to gasoline."

—Renewable Fuels Association, a trade association for the US ethanol industy.

Renewable Fuels Association, "Building Bridges to a More Sustainable Future: 2011 Ethanol Industry Outlook," February 2011.

Biofuels are a clean, efficient, environmentally friendly source of fuel. Biofuels can help the world reduce greenhouse gas emissions and, as a result, reduce global warming.

The burning of fossil fuels releases carbon dioxide gas into the atmosphere, which is one of the most common greenhouse gases and is widely believed to contribute to global warming. One of the largest sources of carbon dioxide emissions is the millions of cars, trucks, and airplanes on the road and in the air. According to a 2011 report by the International Energy Agency, the transportation sector contributed 23 percent of worldwide carbon dioxide emissions from fossil fuel combustion in 2009. Of those emissions, road vehicles such as cars and trucks accounted for the vast majority of carbon dioxide emissions. The problem is expected to get worse; the IEA predicts that global demand for road transport will rise 40 percent by 2035.

Biofuels Reduce Greenhouse Gases

Using biofuels can help reduce the amount of carbon dioxide in the atmosphere. When burned, biofuels emit less carbon dioxide than gasoline. An analysis by the DOE's Argonne National Laboratory found that the

13 billion gallons (49.2 billion L) of ethanol used in 2010 helped reduce greenhouse gas emissions from vehicles by 21.9 million tons (19.9 million metric tons). This is equal to removing 3.5 million cars and trucks from the road.

Although biofuels and gasoline both release carbon dioxide into the atmosphere when burned, the process of plant growth essentially cancels out any carbon emitted by biofuel vehicles. The plants and trees used to make biofuels absorb carbon dioxide from the atmosphere during photosynthesis, a chemical process by which plants produce energy to grow. When biofuel is burned, it returns the recently absorbed carbon dioxide to the atmosphere. In this way, biofuels recycle the carbon dioxide and are considered carbon neutral. In contrast, the burning of fossil fuels emits carbon dioxide from plants buried deep within the earth. Because these plants died millions of years ago, the carbon they absorbed has been absent from the atmosphere for millions of years. When fossil fuel use releases this carbon today, it adds to the total amount of carbon dioxide currently in the atmosphere.

Because fossil fuels such as natural gas and coal are used in the production and distribution of biofuels, biofuels are not completely carbon neutral. Yet even factoring in these carbon emissions, biofuels are still better for the atmosphere than fossil fuels. According to the DOE, using corn ethanol for fuel reduces greenhouse gas emissions approximately 20 percent as compared with gasoline.

Advanced biofuels such as cellulosic ethanol will lead to significantly higher reductions of greenhouse gases in the future. According to the DOE, cellulosic ethanol reduces greenhouse gases 86 percent compared with gasoline. The increased reduction happens because the processing of cellulosic ethanol uses virtually no fossil fuels. Instead of natural gas or coal, waste biomass called lignin can be burned to generate heat for advanced biofuel processing. Less amounts of fossil fuels and chemicals are needed to grow and harvest cellulosic biomass compared with first-generation crops such as corn, further reducing greenhouse gas emissions. Cellulosic crops such as switchgrass also store carbon in the soil through their roots, which removes even more carbon dioxide from the atmosphere. "Advanced biofuels are the lowest carbon fuels being developed in the marketplace; far and away less carbon intensive than electricity, natural gas and even hydrogen fuel cells,"[26] says Brooke Coleman, executive director of the Advanced Ethanol Council.

Better Air Quality

Biofuels have other environmental benefits, including reducing harmful air pollutants that reach the atmosphere through fuel evaporation or burning. Burning gasoline releases toxic pollutants, including particulate matter, nitrogen oxides, and sulfur dioxide. These pollutants have been linked to smog, acid rain, and human illnesses. According to the Environmental Protection Agency (EPA), the air toxins emitted from gasoline-burning cars and trucks are responsible for approximately half of all cancers caused by air pollution.

> "Advanced biofuels are the lowest carbon fuels being developed in the marketplace; far and away less carbon intensive than electricity, natural gas and even hydrogen fuel cells."[26]
>
> —Brooke Coleman, executive director of the Advanced Ethanol Council.

In comparison, biofuels are a clean-burning energy source. Biofuels contain no sulfur and have low carbon monoxide, particulate, and toxic emissions. According to the DOE, the use of an 85 percent ethanol-gasoline blended fuel would produce fewer total toxins compared with gasoline, including a 40 percent reduction in carbon monoxide, 20 percent reduction in particulate emissions, and 10 percent reduction in nitrogen oxide emissions. Another common biofuel, biodiesel, reduces air toxins by 90 percent and particulate matter by 40 percent, and significantly reduces particles linked to cancer, according to the National Biodiesel Board. "With biodiesel, America can produce its own cleaner-burning diesel alternative that helps clean up the air with existing vehicles. Biodiesel is a natural solution to help achieve lung associations' goals to reduce air pollution and safeguard our health,"[27] says Joe Jobe, National Biodiesel Board CEO.

No Threat of Toxic Spills

Among the many risks of fossil fuel use is the potential for toxic spills. Fossil fuel spills and leaks have caused significant environmental damage. One of the biggest oil spills in US history occurred in April 2010, when an explosion on the *Deepwater Horizon* oil rig sent millions of barrels of crude oil flowing into the Gulf of Mexico. When oil spills into oceans and rivers and on land, it can have devastating effects on the environment. Animals die, coastal wetlands erode, plants wither, and humans get sick. "Oil spills and the dumping of oil into waterways has been extensive, often poisoning drinking water and destroying vegetation,"[28] says a spokesperson for Nosdra, Nigeria's national oil-spill detection and response agency.

Because biofuel is biodegradable, it is much less toxic to the environment if spilled. In general, biofuel degrades rapidly in soil, groundwater, and surface water and quickly breaks down into nontoxic compounds. "One of the areas of fuel ethanol that we have failed to really promote has been the fact that our fuel is totally biodegradable,"[29] says Dave Vander, a board member of the ethanol advocacy group Growth Energy.

The 2004 explosion of the T/V *Bow Mariner*, a chemical tanker carrying ethanol, illustrates how ethanol is safer for the environment than fossil fuels when an accident happens. While carrying a cargo of 3.2 million gallons (12.1 million L) of ethanol, the tanker exploded 50 miles (80.5km) off the Virginia coast. According to Coast Guard officials, all of the ethanol released in the accident dissipated quickly and was not a threat to the surrounding environment, humans, or marine life.

Added Benefits of Energy Crops

The low-cost, low-maintenance crops used for advanced biofuels have benefits that no other energy source can offer. They can improve soil quality, reduce soil erosion from water and wind, filter pollutants from runoff, and provide habitat for wildlife. What is more, energy crops such as switchgrass do not need to displace food crops, nor do they require additional farmland. If the two are planted in rotation, existing farmland

All biofuels produce fewer greenhouse gas emissions that gasoline but some show more reductions than others. The amount of reduction varies by feedstock and type of energy used for processing. Greenhouse gas emissions have been identified as a leading cause of global warming so reduced emissions are an important environmental benefit of biofuels.

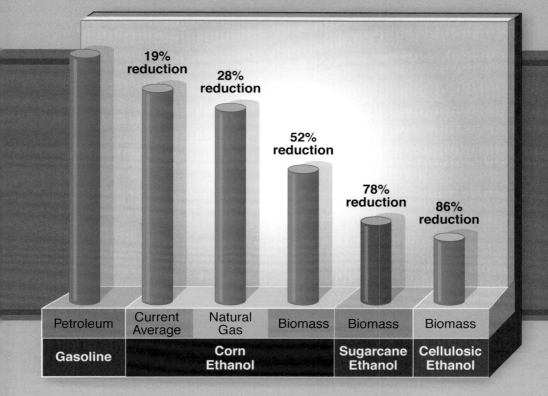

Source: US Department of Energy, "Biomass Basics: The Facts About Bioenergy," www1.eere.energy.gov.

can support both food and energy crops. Because energy crops can grow in nutrient-depleted, compacted, poorly drained and eroded soils, they can also be planted on marginal or abandoned lands that are unsuitable for growing food. "Although switchgrass will grow on a range of soils and terrain, one of its greatest attributes is being able to grow on poor soils; those with low fertility, low pH, droughty, slope, flood prone, etc,"[30] says

Ray Smith, a University of Kentucky forage extension specialist who is studying switchgrass as an energy source.

Energy crops such as native grasses are also better for the environment because they require less energy and effort to grow and harvest. Energy crops that are native to a region often need less fertilizer and pesticide to grow and produce high yields. These crops are also hardy and resistant to floods, droughts, and pests. Once planted, grasses such as switchgrass, big bluestem, and other varieties grow quickly and can be harvested for up to 10 years before they need to be replanted.

Some energy crops can also slow soil erosion and act as a filter for pollution. Many native grasses have deep root systems which help them survive conditions on their native prairies. When planted with traditional row crops, the deep roots of these grasses slow soil erosion. The deep roots of some energy crops also act as a filter for runoff from fields planted with traditional row crops. When planted along streams and wetlands, switchgrass can act as a buffer by filtering soil particles, pesticides, and fertilizer residues from surface water before they reach groundwater or streams.

Fields of native grasses grown for biofuel feedstock can also provide a natural habitat for many species. Animals such as deer, rabbits, wild turkey, quail, and pheasants can make their homes in areas where native grasses grow. In all these ways, biofuel energy crops enhance the environment in which they are grown.

> "One of the areas of fuel ethanol that we have failed to really promote has been the fact that our fuel is totally biodegradable."[29]
>
> —Dave Vander, a board member of ethanol advocacy group Growth Energy.

Biofuels Harm the Environment

"We might as well just burn petrol or diesel rather than biofuels because the net greenhouse gas emissions are not going to be any different."

—Susan Page, head of the Physical Geography Department at the University of Leicester in Britain.

EurActiv.com, "Doubts Cast on Biofuels' Air Quality Claims," November 15, 2011. www.euractiv.com.

Biofuel's environmental benefits have been overstated, and in some cases biofuels can harm the environment. In theory, generating energy from plants is appealing, as biofuels are considered carbon-neutral because plants grown for biofuel absorb carbon dioxide from the atmosphere, which is then emitted when biofuel is burned. In reality, production of biofuels is more complicated. The Natural Resources Defense Council warns that "while some biofuels reduce pollution, others pollute more than the oil they replace."[31]

Carbon Savings Overstated

Biofuel's carbon-saving ability has been overstated because it does not fully account for carbon emissions released during the processing and transport of biofuels. The conversion process burns fossil fuels to heat biofuel plant matter. Tractors emit pollutants when harvesting biofuel crops. Trucks and trains burn fossil fuels and emit carbon dioxide and pollutants as they transport feedstock and biofuels. When carbon emissions released during these processes are considered, biofuel's net carbon savings decrease. "It really doesn't produce a large net carbon reduction in the end,"[32] says Bill Brady, CEO of Mascoma, a biofuels company.

Growing first-generation biofuel crops requires nitrogen fertilizers, which add to carbon and greenhouse gases released into the atmosphere. According to a 2008 study by Germany's Max Planck Institute and the

Scripps Research Institute in California, nitrogen fertilizers used for bio-fuel crops release enough nitrous oxide to cause climate warming. "Fertilizer production is very energy intensive. It produces large amounts of nitrous oxide, which is 300 times stronger than carbon dioxide. So if you're moving over to these fuels that use the corn stalk supposedly to cut back your greenhouse emissions, then it's very counterproductive,"[33] says Jim Thomas, a researcher with the ETC Group, an international organization that supports sustainability and conservation.

Indirect Land Use Changes

Also counterproductive are the indirect land use changes that typically occur when land previously used for food crops is shifted to crops intended for biofuels. Shifting US corn crops from food to biofuel production, for example, reduces the world supply of edible corn and increases corn's market prices. As farmers in other countries realize they can now make more money growing corn, they might clear forest land to plant new corn crops.

It is a well-established fact that clear-cutting forests adds to the planet's greenhouse gases. Forests are often cleared through burning, which produces large amounts of carbon dioxide. And once trees are cut down they can no longer absorb carbon dioxide from the atmosphere. According to the EPA, expanding corn ethanol production would actually increase greenhouse gas emissions over a 20-year period. Stanford researcher Holly Gibbs explains that the carbon debt incurred from cutting down a tropical forest could take centuries to repay through savings from biofuel use. "If biofuels are grown in place of forests, we're actually going to end up emitting a huge amount of carbon. When trees are cut down to make room for new farmland, they are usually burned, sending their stored carbon to the atmosphere as carbon dioxide. That creates what's called a carbon debt. This is because the carbon lost from deforestation is much greater

> "While some biofuels reduce pollution, others pollute more than the oil they replace."[31]
>
> —Natural Resources Defense Council.

than the carbon saved from using the current-generation biofuels,"[34] says Gibbs.

In October 2011 a group of 150 scientists and economists called for the European Commission to recognize and account for the impact of indirect land use changes when evaluating biofuel's impact on greenhouse gas emissions. The scientists write, "All the studies of land use change indicate that the emissions related to biofuels expansion are significant and can be quite large."[35]

Biofuels Are Land Intensive

Not only are the air quality benefits of biofuels questionable, growing biofuel crops requires a significant investment in land resources. According to a 2010 Rutgers University study of renewable energy sources, biofuels are the most land intensive of all renewable energy sources. The study concluded that meeting 100 percent of the world's energy needs with sugarcane ethanol would require nearly three times the amount of current farmland. Corn or cellulosic ethanol would require even more land, and biodiesel made from soy was the most land intensive of all. "We would have to double the amount of the Earth's land area that we currently devote to human purposes to get energy from any bio sources so it's just not going to happen. For 10 percent, maybe a niche market, but don't count on them for broad solutions,"[36] says Thomas.

Water Supply and Quality

The impact of biofuels on water supply and quality is also a concern. Production of first-generation biofuels uses a significant amount of water, with biofuel plants consuming approximately 3 gallons (11.4 L) of water for each gallon (3.8 L) of ethanol produced. According to the National Academy of Sciences, a biofuel plant producing 100 million gallons (378.5 million L) annually uses as much water as a town of 5,000 people. Much of that water is drawn from local water sources that are needed for drinking water and other uses. "It can be a very local problem. If an ethanol plant is withdrawing groundwater from major pumping wells,

Biofuel Production Linked to Gulf Dead Zone

Nitrogen-based fertilizer used on corn crops grown in the Midwest is causing environmental damage in the Gulf of Mexico. Midwestern corn is the main feedstock for US ethanol production. Researchers say the fertilizer leaches from midwestern croplands into the Mississippi River, which in turn flows into the Gulf of Mexico. There the fertilizer feeds giant algae blooms that consume oxygen and suffocate marine life, a process that has created an ocean dead zone the size of New Jersey.

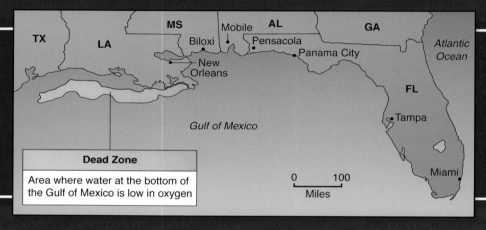

Source: Carolyn Lochhead, "Dead Zone in Gulf Linked to Ethanol Production," *San Francisco Chronicle*, July 6, 2010. www.sfgate.com.

they can have a deleterious effect on local wells,"[37] says Craig Cox, senior vice president for agriculture and natural resources for the Environmental Working Group.

Biofuel water use is even higher when crop irrigation is considered. Corn crops require a significant amount of water. According to the US Department of Agriculture, an average of 784 gallons (2,967 L) of water was used to irrigate corn per gallon (per 3.8 L) of ethanol. This translates into more than 9,000 gallons (34,000 L) of water per million Btu of energy produced from ethanol. In contrast, crude oil production and refining requires significantly less water—anywhere between 1 gallon (3.8 L) and 2,500 gallons (9,464 L) of water per million Btu of energy produced. "There's too much attention on water usage by ethanol plants, while the much bigger elephant is irrigation,"[38] says Sangwon Suh, a researcher at the University of Minnesota studying biofuel's impact on water resources.

Biofuel production has also been linked to water pollution. Although the fuel itself is biodegradable, fertilizers used to grow biofuel feedstocks can pollute water resources. Corn farming for ethanol, in particular, is a significant source of water pollution connected to biofuel production. According to a 2007 report from the National Academy of Sciences, corn requires more fertilizer and pesticides than other biofuel feedstocks. Rain washes these fertilizers and pesticides from farmland into nearby streams and rivers. Eventually, streams and rivers carry the contaminants to other bodies of water. The pollutants can have a serious effect on water habitats. Nitrogen fertilizers decrease water's oxygen level, which stunts plant growth and suffocates fish. This creates a dead zone in affected waters.

In the United States, nitrogen fertilizers used in midwestern corn farming are thought to be key factors in growing dead zones in the Gulf of Mexico and along the Atlantic Coast. The fertilizer runs into the Mississippi River and then into the gulf, where it feeds giant algae blooms. As the algae die, they fall to the ocean floor and decay. The decaying blooms deplete ocean oxygen, a condition called hypoxia. Without sufficient oxygen, ocean plants and animals suffocate. Since the 1980s the gulf's dead zone has doubled in size; it measured approximately 6,500 square miles (16,835 sq. km) in 2011. "More nitrate comes off corn fields than it does off of any other crop by far. And nitrogen is driving the formation of the dead zone,"[39] says Gene Turner, a zoologist at Louisiana State University. Increased production of corn ethanol will only increase water pollution and dead zones in the future.

> **"We would have to double the amount of the Earth's land area that we currently devote to human purposes to get energy from any bio sources so it's just not going to happen. For 10 percent, maybe a niche market, but don't count on them for broad solutions."[36]**
>
> —Jim Thomas, a researcher with the ETC Group, an international organization that supports sustainability and conservation.

Biodiversity at Risk

The push to clear land for biofuel crops harms the world's biodiversity. Biodiversity is the enormous variety of life on earth. It includes all of the plants, animals, fungi, and other living things in an area. When land is cleared to plant biofuel feedstocks, habitats are destroyed, endangering the plants and animals that live there.

In 2011 the EPA released a draft report on biofuels and the environment, which found that increased biofuel production could negatively affect wildlife and habitats when habitats are altered to grow biofuel feedstocks. The report also notes risks to plants and animals from exposure to pesticides and nutrient runoff into waters and other harmful effects from biofuel production.

The world's rain forests are particularly vulnerable to the damage caused by increasing crop-growing areas to meet rising demand for biofuel production. Rain forests are some of the most biodiverse places on earth and are home to about half of all known plant and animal species. Land clearing to grow biofuel plants is a serious threat to biodiversity in these areas. Many species cannot survive after their homes are destroyed. A 2009 study by researchers at Stanford University's Wood Institute for the Environment found that between 1980 and 2000, more than half of new cropland came from intact rain forests and another 30 percent from disturbed forests. "This is a major concern for the global environment. As we look toward biofuels to help reduce climate change we must consider the rainforests and savannas that may lie in the pathway of expanding biofuel cropland,"[40] says Gibbs.

Chapter Three

Can Biofuels Ever Replace Fossil Fuels?

Biofuels Can Reduce Fossil Fuel Use

Biofuels are a renewable, domestically produced alternative fuel that can reduce worldwide use of fossil fuels. Biofuels can be used in place of fossil fuels in many energy applications, including transportation, electricity production, and heating. Biofuel can be generated and stored for future use, making it a reliable source of energy 24 hours a day. As technology improves, biofuel supplies will increase, allowing it to replace even more fossil fuels in the coming years.

The Debate

Biofuels Are Not a Viable Replacement for Fossil Fuels

Biofuels are not a viable replacement for fossil fuels. Current biofuel technology and production facilities are not able to produce enough biofuels to meet world energy demands, and the repeated failures of advanced biofuels to meet production targets indicate that they will likely be unable to replace fossil fuels in the future. In addition, limited market demand and distribution infrastructure for biofuel will hinder production and make it difficult for consumers to find and use significant amounts of biofuel now and in the future.

Biofuels Can Reduce Fossil Fuel Use

"With more research and incentives, we can break our dependence on oil with biofuels."

—Barack Obama, forty-fourth president of the United States.

Barack Obama, "State of the Union Address, 2011," January 25, 2011. www.whitehouse.gov.

Biofuels have the potential to reduce world fossil fuel use. Fossil fuels, including natural gas, oil, and coal, provide the bulk of the world's energy for cars, electricity, and heating. Historically, fossil fuels have been an easy-to-use and reliable energy source. A major problem with fossil fuels, however, is that they are not renewable resources. Once used, fossil fuels cannot be replaced. Some experts believe that the world has already reached peak production for fossil fuels or will reach it shortly. As fossil fuel reserves are depleted they will become more expensive. As a result, it will cost more to drive cars, heat homes, and purchase products manufactured with fossil fuels.

As world energy demand increases, fossil fuels will be depleted at faster rates. According to estimates from the DOE, the worldwide demand for energy will rise by more than 50 percent in the next 20 years. In addition, the number of cars that use petroleum-based liquid fuels is predicted to double by 2050. "Current sources of energy—from petroleum—will likely be inadequate to meet this [energy] demand. In fact, there is only one viable alternative source of liquid transportation fuel, which is direct fermentation from sugar,"[41] says Alan Shaw.

A Key Source of Renewable Energy

Unlike fossil fuels, biofuels are considered renewable because the plants that biofuels are made from can be grown over and over again. In contrast, fossil fuels are the product of plants that have decomposed over millions of years; once they are used up they disappear forever.

Renewable biofuels can be used in place of fossil fuels in transportation, electricity production, and heating. Unlike other renewable energy sources, such as solar and wind power, which are dependent on weather conditions or time of day, biofuels are available 24 hours a day. And, once made, biofuels can be stored for future use. Biofuels can also be turned into a liquid fuel that can be used in cars, planes, and other vehicles. "America cannot meet its energy needs without a mix of fuels that include renewable solutions like advanced biofuels. . . . We can help America become less dependent on foreign oil,"[42] says Adam Monroe, president of Novozymes North, an industrial biotechnology company.

Biofuels in Transportation

Of all the possible future uses of biofuels, their most promising use is as a replacement for oil in the transportation sector. According to British Petroleum's *2010 Statistical Review of World Energy*, oil consumption accounted for 34 percent of the world's primary energy usage in 2010, increasing 3.1 percent over the prior year. Most oil is used in the transportation sector, fueling the world's cars, trucks, ships, and airplanes. In the United States, transportation accounted for more than 70 percent of the total US petroleum demand, consuming over 14 million barrels per day. With more cars and airplanes in use, demand is expected to rise even further.

Biofuels such as ethanol and biodiesel are already replacing oil in the transportation sector. According to the International Energy Agency, biofuels provide about 2 percent of total world transport fuel today. In the United States, ethanol producers provided an estimated 13 billion gallons (49.2 billion L) of domestic biofuel in 2010, according to the Renewable Fuels Association. Blended into gasoline at the pumps, ethanol replaced about 445 million barrels of imported oil.

Biofuel production in the United States is expected to grow steadily in the coming years. "Ethanol producers continue to innovate, expand, and improve the process by which they now provide the nation with

10 percent of its gasoline demand. New technologies are on the cusp of commercialization, promising to dramatically expand this industry's ability to meet the nation's growing need for energy with a renewable alternative,"[43] says Bob Dinneen, Renewable Fuels Association president and CEO.

In testimony before the US Senate in 2012, Howard Gruenspecht, the acting administrator of the Energy Information Administration, predicted that more than 1 million barrels per day of biofuel would be consumed primarily by transportation in the United Stated by 2024. "We will become less dependent on fossil fuels and will become more dependent on fuels made from the sugars and chemicals found in plants,"[44] says Jack Saddler, a biofuel expert and professor at the University of British Columbia.

Potential for Biopower

Biofuels are also a promising source of power for electricity and heat in the future. Currently, fossil fuels generate most US power, with coal being the most common fuel for generating electricity. In 2010, 45 percent of the nation's almost 4 trillion kilowatt-hours of electricity used coal as its energy source. Natural gas and oil generated 24 percent and 1 percent of electricity, respectively.

> "We will become less dependent on fossil fuels and will become more dependent on fuels made from the sugars and chemicals found in plants."[44]
>
> —Jack Saddler, a biofuel expert and professor at the University of British Columbia.

Biofuel is a reliable source of power that is well suited to providing a dependable flow of electricity 24 hours a day, seven days a week. Unlike wind and solar power, biofuel is not affected by weather conditions or the time of day. This reliability makes biofuel an attractive option for baseload electricity, the minimum amount of electricity demanded by consumers.

The town of Kristianstad, Sweden, is a working example of using biofuel to produce electricity. In the 1990s Kristianstad's 80,000 residents

Biomass Resources Can Meet Future US Energy Needs

A study by the US Department of Energy estimates that the United States has more than enough potential biomass feedstock to meet a significant portion of short-term and long-term energy needs at least to 2030. Using conservative assumptions, more than 1 billion tons of biomass feedstock will be available from forestland, agricultural resources, and energy crops by 2030. This amount will be sufficient to replace 30 percent or more of the country's current petroleum use.

Feedstock	2012	2017	2022	2030
	Million dry tons			
Forest resources currently used	129	182	210	226
Forest biomass and potential	97	98	100	102
Agricultural resources currently used	85	103	103	103
Agricultural biomass and potential	162	192	221	265
Energy crops	0	101	282	400
Total currently used	214	284	312	328
Total potential resources	258	392	602	767
Total	473	676	914	1094

Source: US Department of Energy, "US Billion-Ton Update: Biomass Supply for a Bioenergy and Bioproducts Industry," www.eere.energy.gov.

used oil, natural gas, and coal to heat their homes and businesses. Today a processing plant consumes potato peels, manure, used cooking oil, stale cookies, and pig intestines and transforms this trash into biogas, a form of methane. The biofuel is burned to create heat and electricity. It is also refined into transportation fuel for cars. Kristianstad's biofuel program has become so successful that the town has reduced its overall fossil fuel energy use by 50 percent. In order to reduce fossil fuel use further, city planners have converted municipal vehicles to use biofuel. They are also encouraging private individuals to drive cars that run on locally-produced biofuel.

Biomass Will Generate Power

In the United States, using biomass for electricity and heat is an expanding industry. Biomass such as wood chips, corncobs, and wheat straw can be burned directly at steam-electric power plants or converted into gas that can be burned in steam generators, gas turbines, or internal combustion engine–generators. According to the Washington Forest Protection Agency, more than 80 power facilities in 20 states now generate enough electricity to power 8.5 million homes across the country. In the United States, biomass generates more than 50 billion kilowatt-hours of electricity, providing nearly 1.5 percent of the country's electric sales.

In October 2011 the Gainesville Renewable Energy Center biomass facility opened in Florida. When fully operational in 2013, it will be one of the country's largest biomass facilities, with the capacity to generate 100 megawatts of electricity, enough to power 70,000 homes. "It is truly thrilling to witness the grand opening of what will become one of the largest biomass facilities in the country," says Bob Cleaves, president and CEO of the Biomass Power Association. "This facility will use tons of local wood waste that would otherwise have ended up in a landfill to produce clean, reliable energy."[45]

Improved Technology Will Increase Biofuel Supplies

New and improved technologies will increase the supply of biofuel, making it widely available in the future. Scientists are researching methods to convert crops and residues into biofuel more efficiently and to get more energy from each plant. These improvements could significantly increase worldwide biofuel production.

At the National Renewable Energy Laboratory (NREL), scientists are investigating ways to pretreat cellulose in advanced biofuel feedstocks. Pretreatment would make it easier to break down the cellulose in advanced feedstocks and increase the amount of sugar and biofuel obtained during the conversion process. NREL scientists are also investigating enzymes to break down cellulose, converting it into more sugar at a faster rate, using fewer and cheaper enzymes. Other scientists are studying microorganisms that can break down cellulose into sugars and then ferment those sugars into ethanol. Using these microorganisms, the costly conversion process could be turned into a simple, one-step process called consolidated bioprocessing. Says secretary of energy Steven Chu:

> America's oil dependence . . . won't be solved overnight. But the remarkable advance of science and biotechnology in the past decade puts us on the precipice of a revolution in biofuels. In fact, biotechnologies, and the biological sciences that provide the underlying foundation, are some of the most rapidly developing areas in science and technology today—and the United States is leading the way. In the coming years, we can expect dramatic breakthroughs that will allow us to produce the clean energy we need right here at home.[46]

In 2011 the DOE released a report detailing the US biomass feedstock potential. Currently, the United States produces 473 million dry tons (429 million metric tons) of biomass annually. The report found that by 2030 US biomass resources could be increased to nearly 1.1 billion dry tons (1 billion metric tons) annually by technology advances and conservation practices that would dramatically increase crop yields. This amount of feedstock could produce 85 billion gallons (322 billion L) of biofuel, enough to replace approximately 30 percent of the country's petroleum consumption. "If we are going to reduce our dependence on fossil fuels and, especially on those that we import from overseas, we're going to need to continue to pursue a range of cleaner and more secure sources of energy. Advanced biofuels are central to this effort,"[47] says US senator Christopher Coons.

"If we are going to reduce our dependence on fossil fuels and, especially on those that we import from overseas, we're going to need to continue to pursue a range of cleaner and more secure sources of energy. Advanced biofuels are central to this effort."[47]

—US senator Christopher Coons.

Biofuels Are Not a Viable Replacement for Fossil Fuels

"Thirty years from now, the American economy will still be dependent on the most affordable, efficient fuel sources available—oil, coal, and natural gas."

—Thomas J. Pyle, president, Institute for Energy Research.

Thomas J. Pyle, "Just Look at the Numbers," *National Energy Journal*, March 8, 2011. http://energy.national journal.com.

With current production technologies, biofuels cannot be generated in large enough quantities to replace fossil fuels in a significant way. In addition, emerging production technologies are too unproven and costly to rely on biofuel as a replacement for fossil fuels in the future. Biofuels also have a limited distribution infrastructure, which makes the fuel hard to find and expensive. Because biofuels cannot produce commercial quantities at a competitive price, they are not a good replacement for fossil fuels now or in the future. "We can all make a little bit of something. But you have got to make a lot of it, and you have got to make it cheaply,"[48] says Frances Arnold, a professor of chemical engineering and biochemistry at the California Institute of Technology.

Insufficient Quantities

Although the production of biofuel has increased over the past decade, it is not growing fast enough. Biofuel remains a tiny fraction of overall energy produced and consumed in the United States and around the world. According to the NREL, the United States used 98 quadrillion Btus of energy in 2010. Of that, 83 percent came from oil, coal, and natural gas. Biofuels contributed only 4.3 percent of energy consumed. "When you look at what our ethanol production is and compare that against what our demand for transportation fuels is, we won't get there,"[49] says Virginia Lacy, a biofuels consultant at the Rocky Mountain Institute, a nonprofit energy policy organization.

The world demand for energy is expected to increase, with consumption projected to rise by 36 percent by 2035. Several factors are driving the increase in energy demand. The world population is projected to grow 25 percent in the next 20 years. In addition, people use more energy as standards of living improve in many countries. In developed countries people are consuming more energy as they drive cars farther, live in bigger homes, and use an expanding array of electronic devices.

Biofuels cannot meet current energy needs, and they will likely fall even further behind in the future as energy demand increases. According to analysts from energy company Chevron, "Fossil fuels will continue to provide the majority of the world's energy supplies for decades to come. Even under the most aggressive climate policy scenario presented by the International Energy Agency, fossil fuels are still expected to contribute at least 50 percent of the world's energy supplies in 2035."[50]

> "When you look at what our ethanol production is and compare that against what our demand for transportation fuels is, we won't get there."[49]
>
> —Virginia Lacy, a biofuels consultant at the Rocky Mountain Institute, a nonprofit energy policy organization.

Availability of land is one factor that limits the production of biofuel now and in the future. Significant areas of land are needed to grow crops like corn, sugar, wheat, and soy that currently provide most of the feedstock for biofuels. According to Exxon Mobil, corn generates only about 250 gallons (946 L) of biofuel per acre (per 0.4 ha) annually. Crops with higher yields, such as sugarcane and palm, result in only 450 gallons (1,703 L) and 650 gallons (2,460 L) per acre, respectively. At these yields, there is simply not enough available land to produce the quantities of biofuels needed to replace fossil fuels. In October 2010 the Congressional Research Service reported that if the entire US

Biomass Falls Far Short in US Energy Picture

In 2010 biomass supplied only a fraction of US energy needs. The largest and most important energy sources by far were coal, natural gas, and oil. Given these circumstances, it seems unlikely that biofuels will replace fossil fuels in any meaningful way in the near or even far future.

US Energy Production (2010): 74.9 Quadrillion Btu

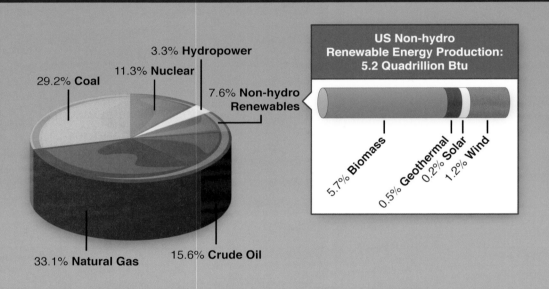

Source: US Department of Energy, *2010 Renewable Energy Data Book,* 2011. www.eere.energy.gov.

corn crop of 2009 were used to make ethanol, it would replace only 18 percent of the country's gasoline consumption. The researchers concluded that expanding corn-based ethanol to significantly reduce fossil fuel use would not be feasible. J. Craig Venter, cofounder of Synthetic Genomics, a company researching algae-based biofuels, contends that replacing all US transportation fuels with corn ethanol would require a farm three times the size of the continental United States.

Limited Demand

Even if enough land were available to significantly increase biofuel production, biofuel use is limited by consumer demand. Most consumers have little need for ethanol; the only reason they buy it is that many service stations today sell an ethanol-gasoline blend. Currently, the amount of ethanol blended with gasoline is restricted to 10 percent (E10) by the EPA. According to EPA estimates, the E10 cap allows ethanol to replace only about 9.2 percent of the nation's gasoline supply, or up to about 14 billion to 15 billion gallons (53 billion to 57 billion L) annually. Higher-level ethanol blends such as E85 require the use of special FFVs, which few consumers own. Until widespread usage of higher ethanol blends is allowed or more drivers convert to FFVs that use higher ethanol blends, ethanol will be able to replace only a small percentage of the oil demanded by the transportation sector.

If higher levels of ethanol blends are approved for use in conventional cars, the impact on fossil fuel use will be minimal. In 2010 the EPA approved the use of a 15 percent ethanol blend (E15) in vehicles made after 2007 and expanded it the following year to include vehicles made after 2001. In total, E15 would be available for about two-thirds of cars on US highways. Although this represents a potential 33 percent increase in the ethanol market, it is still far from replacing fossil fuels.

In addition, even though the EPA has approved a 15 percent ethanol blend, several barriers stand in the way of its use. Most engine and automobile manufacturers do not warrant their machines if customers use ethanol blends higher than 10 percent because of concerns over potential equipment damage. Gasoline retailers also substantially resist carrying E15 fuel because they would have to remove existing pumps and replace them with new pumps for the E15 fuel. Most gas stations would also have to install new underground tanks, experts say.

With these barriers to use, biofuels' replacing fossil fuels now or in the future is difficult to envision. According to John Eichberger, a spokesman for the National Association of Convenience Stores, which represents 115,000 of the about 160,000 locations in the United States that sell gasoline, the basic problem with E15 and higher-blend ethanol fuels is that even if a supply of biofuel is available, it will be difficult to use because "we don't have a retail infrastructure that can handle the product, we don't have consumers ready to buy it, and we don't have the auto industry ready to approve the use in their cars."[51]

Advanced Biofuels Cannot Meet Production Targets

Although much research has gone into advanced biofuel, no one has been able to produce it on a commercial scale. According to science journalist Rachel Ehrenberg, "Getting a lot of ethanol out of a benchtop flask is one thing. Scaling up to a silo-sized bioreactor is another."[52] Because the biofuel industry has not been able to deliver on advanced biofuels and shows little promise of doing so in the near future, biofuel will not be a significant factor in replacing fossil fuels.

To date, the biofuel industry has struggled to solve technology problems and meet production targets. In 2007 Congress set a goal of 500 million gallons (1,893 million L) of advanced cellulosic ethanol to be produced in 2012. In 2011 the government announced that it was reducing the 2012 target to just 8.65 million gallons (32.7 million L). The "EPA has essentially reduced the mandate for cellulosic, recognizing the fact that there aren't supplies out there to meet it,"[53] says US Department of Agriculture chief economist Joe Glauber.

> "EPA has essentially reduced the mandate for cellulosic, recognizing the fact that there aren't supplies out there to meet it."[53]
>
> —Joe Glauber, US Department of Agriculture chief economist.

Looking forward, experts question whether the advanced biofuel industry will be able to produce enough fuel commercially by 2022, when the Renewable Fuel Standard calls for the industry to produce 16 billion gallons (60.6 billion L) of cellulosic biofuel annually. "Although the situation is uncertain, EIA's [the Energy Information Administration's] present view of the projected rates of technology development and market penetration of cellulosic biofuel technologies suggests that available quantities of cellulosic biofuels will be insufficient to meet the renewable fuel standard (RFS) targets for cellulosic biofuels legislated in EISA 2007 [the 2007 Energy Independence and Security Act] before 2022,"[54] says Richard Newell, administrator of the EIA.

Many companies have failed to deliver on promises of advanced biofuels. Range Fuels Inc. was once seen as one of the great hopes for cellulosic biofuel. Range claimed that it would build the country's first commercial cellulosic plant in Georgia. It planned to use wood chips to produce 20 million gallons (75.7 million L) annually by 2008, with a production goal of 100 million gallons (378.5 million L) annually. Investors jumped in, giving the company more than $160 million in financing, plus the company received an additional $162 million in government commitments. Despite its promises, Range found that producing cellulosic ethanol was more difficult than it had anticipated. By the end of 2008 the Range plant was still not operational. By 2010 Range announced that it would finally produce some fuel, but only 4 million gallons (15 million L) of methanol, not cellulosic ethanol. By January 2011 Range Fuels closed its Georgia plant, admitting that the factory had trouble processing the biofuel feedstock, mainly pine scrap. "Their technology did not work. It was a high-risk technological development program. Chemical processing plants just don't scale-up that fast. They were promising too much too quick,"[55] says Sam Shelton, research director for Georgia Tech's Strategic Energy Institute. As Range Fuels demonstrates, biofuels are too unproven and unreliable to depend on as a viable replacement for fossil fuels.

Chapter Four

Should Government Play a Role in Developing Biofuels?

Government Should Have a Role in Biofuel Development

Government has made investments in energy for decades, from subsidizing exploration and extraction of fossil fuels to building nuclear power plants. These investments have helped fledgling industries develop and mature into sustainable, self-sufficient energy alternatives. In the same way, government support of clean energy alternatives such as biofuel will help the world meet its energy challenges in a renewable, environmentally sound way.

The Debate

Government Should Not Be Involved in Developing Biofuels

Government involvement in the biofuel industry is both unnecessary and harmful. History shows that government involvement in any energy technology frequently has negative effects. Biofuel technology will develop more effectively in the free market, where market forces will decide whether it is a viable source of energy. Previous government attempts to subsidize the energy and biofuel industry have failed, often resulting in negative and unintended consequences.

Government Should Have a Role in Biofuel Development

"Government support has been and should continue to be an essential component in the growth of emerging energy sources, enabling U.S. technology innovation, job creation, and economic expansion."

—Nancy Pfund, managing partner of DBL Investors, a venture capital firm that invests in renewable energy ventures.

DBL Investors, "Subsidies to New Energy Sources Are at Lowest Point in U.S. History," September 23, 2011. www.dblinvestors.com.

Biofuels are a promising energy source. They are renewable, environmentally friendly, and reduce the country's dependence on imported oil. Biofuels also create jobs and bring economic benefits to local communities. Like many new technologies, the biofuel industry needs government support to help it grow into a sustainable, commercial industry.

Governments can support development of the biofuel industry in many ways. Often, governments subsidize research and development efforts through grants and loans to researchers. Governments may also offer loans for biofuel plant construction and subsidies to farmers who grow biofuel feedstocks. In Canada, the NextGen Biofuels Fund grants loans for capital expenditures at large-scale biodiesel and cellulosic ethanol production plants. The government fund provides support until private investors are ready to put their money into emerging biofuel technologies.

Another important way governments can support the biofuel industry is through targets, mandates, and blending quotas that create a market demand for biofuels. With any of these tools, the government essentially sets minimum amounts of biofuel that must be purchased and used by oil companies and others, thereby guaranteeing customers for the industry. In Europe, where the main transportation biofuels are bioethanol and biodiesel, the European Renewable Energy Directive requires that 10 percent of transportation fuel must come from renewable sources by 2020.

These measures would create a stable environment for the emerging biofuel industry to develop. "Stability and certainty in the existing government programs are vital to mitigating the risk associated with investing billions of dollars in evolving technology. Investors and developers must see a secure market. . . . A stable framework to support the evolving industry will go a long way to accelerating the industry toward achieving national energy and environmental goals,"[56] says Sue Ellerbusch, president, BP Biofuels North America.

A Level Playing Field

Government support and subsidies are a critical part of establishing a key energy industry. The United States has a long history of supporting emerging industries. "Subsidies and government support have been part of many key industries in U.S. history—railroads, oil, gas and coal, aviation,"[57] says Damien LaVera, a DOE spokesperson. Fossil fuels have received hundreds of billions of dollars in government funding over many years. In the early twentieth century, government money helped support the hydroelectric power industry by contributing to the construction of dams. In addition, the government invested 100 billion tax dollars for the development of nuclear power.

In the United States, the government has supported biofuels by offering subsidies to farmers, tax credits to companies who blend ethanol biofuel into gasoline, and fuel economy credits to automakers who build FFVs that can run on biofuel blends. Congress has also passed legislative mandates that require the use of biofuels. The Energy Policy Act of 2005 established a nationwide renewable fuels standard that required the use of 7.5 billion gallons (28.4 billion L) of renewable fuel by 2012. In 2007 Congress passed the Energy Independence and Security Act, which increased the renewable fuel standard and required the use of 36 billion gallons (136 billion L) of renewable biofuels annually by 2022. Europe has a similar mandate, the European Renewable Energy Directive, which establishes that biofuels should account for at least 10 percent of transport fuel by 2020.

These existing policies have been successful in making the United States the world's largest ethanol producer. Specifically, tax incentives for

Government Subsidies Are Essential

The oil and gas and nuclear industries developed into mature, sustainable industries thanks in large part to generous government subsidies over many decades. The same must be done for the biofuels industry, although the same level of support has not yet materialized.

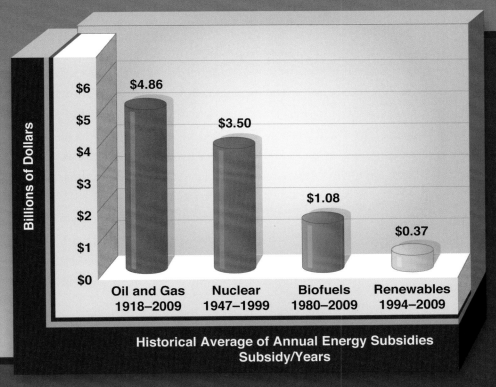

Historical Average of Annual Energy Subsidies
Subsidy/Years

Source: Nancy Pfund and Ben Healy, "What Would Jefferson Do? The Historical Role of Federal Subsidies Shaping America's Energy Future," DBL Investors, September 2011. http://bnet.com.

the use of ethanol have helped build the biofuel market and encouraged private business owners and consumers to invest in infrastructure and sell ethanol blends. "These programs just level the playing field for what oil and gas and nuclear industries have enjoyed for the last 50 years," says Rhone Resch, president of Solar Energy Industries Association. "Do you have to provide more policy support and funding initially? Absolutely. But the result is more energy security, clean energy and domestic jobs."[58]

Creating Stability and Encouraging Investment

Private investment in any new technology is risky, but energy and fuel production is especially challenging because it requires large up-front investments in research and development, building production plants, and distribution networks. These costs act as a barrier for private investors in the biofuel industry. "If industries are not existent, government can help industries get off the ground,"[59] says secretary of the navy Ray Mabus, who supports the development of biofuels for the military.

Support from the government through research and development grants, loan guarantees, and mandates that create a market for biofuels can reduce risks for private investors and encourage them to invest in biofuel development. "The restricted flow of capital is a market barrier to innovative alternative energies and advanced biofuels that requires government action,"[60] says Brent Erickson, executive vice president of the Industrial & Environmental Division of the Biotechnology Industry Organization.

> "Subsidies and government support have been part of many key industries in U.S. history—railroads, oil, gas and coal, aviation."[57]
>
> —Damien LaVera, a spokesman for the DOE.

To encourage biofuel production, the US government announced in 2011 that it would invest up to $510 million over three years to produce advanced aviation and marine biofuels. The plan requires a minimum matching investment of $510 million from private industry. "Our goal is to create and stabilize the advanced biofuels industry,"[61] says secretary of agriculture Tom Vilsack about the plan.

Brazil's biofuel experience demonstrates how government support can develop a robust industry. In 1975 the Brazilian government launched the National Alcohol Program to increase ethanol production as a substitute for gasoline. To develop biofuel supply, the government invested in technology to increase agricultural production, expanded and updated sugar distilleries, and built new production plants. It also granted ethanol subsidies that lowered biofuel prices and reduced taxes for ethanol producers. To create a domestic market for ethanol, the government passed mandatory blending requirements and offered discounts to consumers at the pump. The government also paired with private industry to research technological advances that would improve the growing and processing of sugarcane ethanol. According to Roberto Schaeffer, professor of energy management and policy at the Federal University of Rio de Janeiro, creating the ethanol market was an immense national effort that required a significant financial investment. "The government was criticized at that time, but the fact is that it was a success,"[62] he says. Today, Brazil is a worldwide leader in the ethanol biofuel market.

Government as a Guide for Sustainable Development

Government should also have a role in biofuel development to ensure that biofuels are produced in a sustainable, environmentally friendly way. Biofuels are an attractive replacement for fossil fuels, particularly for transportation. However, if biofuel production increases without appropriate government guidelines, it may result in rising food prices, increased greenhouse gas emissions, deforestation, increased water use, and a loss of biodiversity. A government role will allow the industry to develop responsibly and avoid potential pitfalls.

Several countries have implemented policies to encourage sustainable biofuel production and lessen any negative consequences to the environment or food supply. In Mexico, maize, which is the country's most important staple food crop, has been banned as a feedstock for biofuels. This action ensures it will remain available as part of the country's food supply. In 2008 Brazil implemented agro-ecological zoning laws for sugarcane that protect ecologically significant biomes. Malaysia has announced a ban on forest clearing for oil palm, a tropical plant used in the country's biofuel production.

Government support of advanced biofuels can also minimize some of the environmental problems associated with first-generation biofuels. With specific incentives, the government can guide the industry toward developing more sustainable versions of advanced biofuels that have fewer environmental impacts. "Governments should incentivize the development of new types of biofuels that need less land and produce fewer greenhouse gases, for example by creating research funding programmes or encouraging public-private partnerships,"[63] says Joyce Tait, researcher and professor at Edinburgh University.

To encourage the use of environmentally friendly biofuels, Massachusetts announced new state regulations in 2011 that would impose stricter standards for biofuel projects seeking to qualify for state incentives. The proposed regulations came after a study that suggested that careful regulation was needed to prevent biofuel development from having a negative environmental effect. Environmentalists support the proposed state regulations, saying it would encourage the responsible development of biomass energy. "Massachusetts' new biomass regulations rightly focus on meeting the state's mandate to reduce greenhouse gas emissions," says Sue Reid, vice president and director of the Conservative Law Foundation in Massachusetts. According to Reid, the new regulations prevent biomass power plants from receiving incentives for cutting down trees and burning them for electricity, which would harm forests and increase greenhouse gases in the atmosphere. "But under the new regulations, in order to be eligible for Massachusetts renewable energy incentives, biomass projects will have to demonstrate that they are significantly more efficient and less polluting, and that their fuel supply will not jeopardize our forests,"[64] says Reid.

> "Government action is needed to provide a stable, long-term policy framework for biofuels that allows for sustained investments in biofuel expansion."[65]
>
> —Bo Diczfalusy, the EIA's director of sustainable energy policy and technology.

Government involvement is essential for the future development of biofuels. With government subsidies and loans for up-front capital costs to build production facilities and distribution networks, the biofuel industry will ramp up to commercial scale production in the coming years. "Government action is needed to provide a stable, long-term policy framework for biofuels that allows for sustained investments in biofuel expansion,"[65] says Bo Diczfalusy, the EIA's director of sustainable energy policy and technology.

Government Should Not Be Involved in Developing Biofuels

"Subsidies make sense when they support research into effective renewable energy technologies. But thirty years of subsidies have not made food for fuel competitive or useful."

—Rolf Westgard, energy analyst and educator.

Rolf Westgard, "Should Government Keep Financially Supporting Ethanol? (The Debate 5/23–5/27)," MPR News, May 2011. http://insight.mprnews.org.

In August 2010 Beacon Power became one of the first companies to receive a DOE loan guarantee meant to support innovative and clean energy projects. Beacon Power's promising technology used large flywheels to store power and smooth dangerous electrical surges, which would be critical as fluctuating wind and solar sources provided more electricity. Beacon's technology appeared innovative, yet even with government support it failed to attract private investors. Within a year the company filed for bankruptcy, leaving a debt of $39.1 million to the DOE and another $3.45 million owed to the state of Massachusetts.

As the Beacon Power failure demonstrates, state and federal governments do not have the expertise to determine which industries or businesses are deserving of government support, and they do not have the power to create successful businesses. Governments simply should not be involved in the development of any industry, including the biofuel industry. Although scientists are researching many potential biofuel technologies and feedstocks, it is unknown at present which technologies and feedstocks will succeed, if any. Given these uncertainties, the responsibility of developing the biofuel industry should fall on private companies and private investors. "If a renewable technology makes economic sense, the private sector will adopt it and it will succeed without mandates and subsidies. Federal and state governments should not mandate renewable energy,"[66] says Margo Thorning, chief economist at the American Council for Capital Formation.

Allow Free Market Forces to Work

Free market forces are the most effective way to determine which, if any, biofuel technologies and feedstocks should be brought to market. In the free market, only technologies and feedstocks that are economically viable will succeed. Private investors will fund and support winning technologies, while nonviable biofuel technology will be allowed to fail. Nicolas D. Loris, who researches energy, environment, and regulation issues at the Heritage Foundation, says:

> There are plenty of technologies already developed to promote competition, and the one that emerges to provide a consistently affordable alternative to gasoline won't need the help of the government, because the profits will be enough incentive to drive production and lower costs, which will be enough incentive for the consumer to switch from a car that runs on gasoline to something that is cheaper. . . . Good economic ideas can expand at rapid rates. Getting the government involved only impedes the process."[67]

In order to allow the free market to operate properly, the government should limit its funding of alternative energy sources, including biofuel. Government officials should not be deciding which risky start-up ventures deserve funding. Most officials are not qualified to make scientific and business decisions on which technologies will succeed and should be funded. Bill Montgomery, managing director at Quantum Energy Partners, a private equity firm, believes that government should stay out of funding decisions and limit itself to establishing fair rules to encourage innovation. "We have to accept the limitations of our own intelligence. Let the best technology flourish and win. The role of the government is not to pick winners and losers,"[68] he says.

Failed Government Intervention

Past history shows that government mandates and subsidies frequently do not work as intended. "Several recent bills would either subsidize or mandate alternative fuels and/or vehicles. However, the 30-plus-year history of federal attempts to encourage such alternatives includes numerous failures and few, if any, successes,"[69] write Loris and senior policy analyst in energy and the environment Ben Lieberman, also of the Heritage Foundation.

One recent government energy market failure involved Solyndra, a solar technology company. In 2009 the federal government granted a loan guarantee of $535 million to Solyndra. Some industry experts disagreed with the government's decision to finance Solyndra; they questioned whether the company's technology was competitive against other companies and similar technologies. "To think they could compete on any basis, that took a very big leap of faith,"[70] says solar analyst Ramesh Misra. Two years later, in August 2011, Solyndra declared bankruptcy. "The [Barack] Obama administration wasted $535 million in taxpayer funds in guaranteeing a loan to a firm that has proven to be unviable in the global market,"[71] says Cliff Stearns, US congressman from Florida.

> "If a renewable technology makes economic sense, the private sector will adopt it and it will succeed without mandates and subsidies. Federal and state governments should not mandate renewable energy."[66]
>
> —Margo Thorning, chief economist at the American Council for Capital Formation.

The Solyndra failure demonstrates how the government can err when choosing which alternative energy technologies to fund. With millions of dollars from the government, Solyndra was able to continue operating and spending taxpayer money on a technology that did not work in the marketplace. Without the government's money, the company would likely have gone out of business earlier, saving the millions of dollars spent on a flawed technology that was not ready to be used in the market. "The lesson of Solyndra is that the government does not have the expertise to pick winners in the race to develop new energy sources,"[72] says

William O'Keefe, CEO of the George C. Marshall Institute, a nonprofit scientific and public policy research organization.

Unnecessary Tax Credit

Within the biofuel industry, government intervention has also not worked as intended. The biggest government incentive program for biofuels, the Volumetric Ethanol Excise Tax Credit (VEETC) gave oil companies a tax credit for every gallon of ethanol blended with gasoline. Starting in 2006 the government paid oil companies more than $20 billion under VEETC before ending the program in 2011. The VEETC program was inefficient in several ways. It supported corn ethanol, a fuel that burns less efficiently than gasoline, which in turn raises fuel consumption. VEETC also increased the demand for corn for fuel, artificially raising corn and food prices. Even more wasteful, the VEETC blending credit was unnecessary to encourage ethanol use because oil companies were already required to buy ethanol to meet the Renewable Fuel Standard under the EISA 2007.

By giving billions of dollars in support to corn ethanol, the government encouraged companies to continue producing corn ethanol instead of creating incentives for the research and development of more promising advanced biofuels. Recognizing the failure of this act, a coalition of 90 organizations wrote to members of Congress in 2011 and urged them to allow VEETC to expire at the end of the year. In their letter, the group said that Congress "has the opportunity to end the $6 billion a year subsidy to gasoline refiners who blend corn ethanol into gasoline. At a time of spiraling deficits, we do not believe Congress should continue subsidizing gasoline refiners for something that they are already required to do by the Renewable Fuels Standard."[73]

> "Several recent bills would either subsidize or mandate alternative fuels and/or vehicles. However, the 30-plus-year history of federal attempts to encourage such alternatives includes numerous failures and few, if any, successes."[69]
>
> —Ben Lieberman, senior policy analyst in energy and the environment, and Nicolas D. Loris, research assistant, at the Heritage Foundation.

Government Mandates Do Not Work

Government-mandated goals for production of cellulosic ethanol are a waste of time. Under the 2007 Energy Independence and Security Act, the government has mandated the use of 36 billion gallons of biofuels, including 16 billion gallons of cellulosic biofuel, by 2022. Nothing so far suggests that this will be possible. Even short-term quotas are unrealistic. New EPA quotas for 2012 required the nation's refiners to add 8.65 million gallons of cellulosic ethanol to US fuel supplies, but the biofuel industry has not been able to even come close to that level.

Cellulosic Biofuels: Production Cannot Meet Mandates and Rules

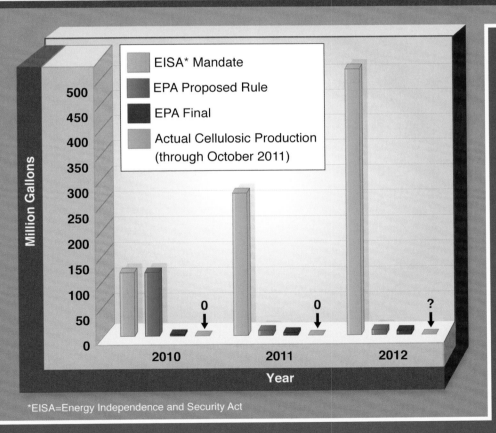

*EISA=Energy Independence and Security Act

Source: Ken Cohen, "Mandating the Impossible: The EPA and Cellulosic Ethanol," Exxon Mobil, January 3, 2012. www.exxonmobilperspectives.com.

The EISA 2007 is another example of ineffective government involvement in biofuel development. The EISA 2007 mandates the production and use of 16 billion gallons (60.6 billion L) of cellulosic biofuel by 2022. The mandate was intended to create a market demand for the cellulosic biofuel. However, the technology to produce cellulosic biofuels has been slow to develop. As a result, cellulosic biofuel supplies remain limited and expensive. Companies have been unable and unwilling to comply with the government mandate. Recognizing the limited supplies of cellulosic biofuel, the government has offered a waiver credit, which companies may purchase instead of using cellulosic biofuel. Because cellulosic biofuels are still expensive, many fuel providers have found it cheaper to buy the waiver credits instead of using cellulosic biofuels.

Subsidies Drive Up Food Prices

Not only do government subsidies not work, they can also have negative consequences in other markets. Around the world, government subsidies of biofuels are driving up food prices. In 2011, 10 international agencies, including the World Bank and World Trade Organization, appealed to the group of 20 major economies (known as the G20), including the United States and Europe, to stop government subsidies of biofuels. The agencies studied the food vs. fuel debate and found that if farmers could sell a crop for more money to the energy market than to the food market, crops would be diverted to biofuel production. This practice increases the price of food. In the report, the scientists urged world governments to reconsider their policies. "G20 governments (should) remove provisions of current national policies that subsidize (or mandate) biofuels production or consumption."[74] The role of government in biofuel development should be limited to ensuring a level playing field for all potential technologies. Then governments should sit on the sidelines and allow free market forces of innovation and competition to determine which biofuels and technologies will be best able to drive the world's energy future. "Like most Americans, we would like to see new sources of renewable domestic fuel sources developed. But we're skeptical of all energy subsidies, in part because of the lessons we've learned from the corn ethanol subsidies that have remained on the books despite their duplicative and wasteful nature—and their persistence even as the industry has matured,"[75] says Ryan Alexander, president of Taxpayers for Common Sense, a nonpartisan watchdog group in Washington, DC.

Government intervention in the form of tax credits, loan guarantees, and other subsidies only serve to prop up technologies and companies that are not viable and serve as a barrier to true market innovation. "We are an energy rich nation and a nation that leads the world in innovation. Private capital, market forces, our abundance of energy and economic and energy realities can lead to the development of new energy sources in time. Trying to force them into the market won't work,"[76] says O'Keefe.

Source Notes

Overview: Visions of the Future: Biofuels

1. Quoted in Denise Luna, "Brazil Opens World's First Ethanol-Fired Power Plant," Reuters, January 19, 2010. www.reuters.com.
2. Quoted in David Lynch, "Brazil Hopes to Build on Its Ethanol Success," *USA Today*, March 28, 2006. www.usatoday.com.
3. Quoted in Nadim Chaudhry, "Advanced Biofuels CEO's Are Gearing Up for the Challenges," *Renewable Energy World*, October 28, 2011. www.renewableenergyworld.com.
4. US Department of Energy, EERE: Biomass Program. www.eere.energy.gov.
5. US Department of Energy, "Ethanol Myths and Facts." www.eere.energy.gov.
6. Quoted in Marianne Lavelle and Bret Schulte, "Is Ethanol the Answer?," *U.S. News & World Report*, February 12, 2007.
7. Quoted in Melinda Wenner, "The Next Generation of Biofuels," *Scientific American: Earth 3.0*, vol. 19, no. 1, 2009, pp. 46–51.
8. John McDonald, "Advanced Biofuels: Great Opportunity, Significant Challenges," The Energy Collective, November 1, 2011. http://theenergycollective.com.

Chapter One: Are Biofuels Affordable?

9. Vinod Khosla, "What Matters in Biofuels & Where Are We?," Khosla Ventures, January 27, 2011. www.khoslaventures.com.
10. ARPA-e, "Department of Energy Awards $156 Million for Groundbreaking Energy Research Projects," press release, September 29, 2011. http://arpa-e.energy.gov.
11. Khosla, "What Matters in Biofuels & Where Are We?"
12. Quoted in Chaudhry, "Advanced Biofuels CEO's Are Gearing Up for the Challenges."

13. Quoted in Chaudhry, "Advanced Biofuels CEO's Are Gearing Up for the Challenges."

14. Frances Williams, "Using Synergies to Save: Cellulosic Ethanol & Power Plant Co-location," *Biofuels Digest*, June 28, 2010. www.biofuelsdigest.com.

15. Natural Resources Defense Council, "Growing Energy: How Biofuels Can Help End America's Oil Dependence," December 2004, p. 4.

16. Wesley K. Clark, "Bringing It All Back Home: Want to Really Fix the Economy? Stop Spending $300 Billion a Year on Foreign Oil, and Invest It Instead in Ethanol and Other Homegrown Fuels," *Washington Monthly*, November/December 2010, p. 26.

17. Quoted in Renewable Fuels Association, "Building Bridges to a More Sustainable Future: 2011 Ethanol Industry Outlook," February 2011, p. 5.

18. McDonald, "Advanced Biofuels."

19. Quoted in David Rotman, "The Price of Biofuels," *Technology Review*, January/February 2008. www.technologyreview.com.

20. Quoted in Elizabeth Rosenthal, "Rush to Use Crops as Fuel Raises Food Prices and Hunger Fears," *New York Times*, April 6, 2011. www.nytimes.com.

21. Quoted in Bryan Walsh, "Why Biofuels Help Push Up World Food Prices," *Time*, February 14, 2011. www.time.com.

22. Quoted in Rosenthal, "Rush to Use Crops as Fuel Raises Food Prices and Hunger Fears."

23. Quoted in Walsh, "Why Biofuels Help Push Up World Food Prices."

24. Quoted in Chaudhry, "Advanced Biofuels CEO's Are Gearing Up for the Challenges."

25. McDonald, "Advanced Biofuels."

Chapter Two: How Do Biofuels Impact the Environment?

26. Quoted in Environmental News Service, "Cellulosic Ethanol Production Far Behind Renewable Fuel Standard," October 11, 2011. www.ens-newswire.com.

27. Quoted in National Biodiesel Board, "Lung Associations Urge More Biodiesel Use to Improve Air Quality," April 30, 2009. www.bio diesel.org.

28. Quoted in John Vidal, "Nigeria's Agony Dwarfs Gulf Oil Spill. The US and Europe Ignore it," *Observer* (London), May 30, 2010. www .guardian.co.uk.

29. Quoted in ICIS.com, "US Ethanol Group Sees Biofuel Opportunity in BP Oil Spill," June 15, 2010. www.icis.com.

30. Quoted in Tim Thornberry, "Switchgrass Proving to Be Good for Farmers, Energy, and Environment," *Business Lexington*, January 11, 2011. www.bizlex.com.

31. Quoted in Natural Resources Defense Council, "Let the VEETC Expire: Moving Beyond Corn Ethanol Means Less Waste, Less Pollution and More Jobs," August 2010. www.nrdc.org.

32. Quoted in Christopher Faille, "Ethanol, the Next Generation: Why Corn Is Out and Cellulose Is In," DailyFinance.com, February 2, 2011. www.dailyfinance.com.

33. Quoted in Loren Grush, "Researchers Debate Whether Biofuels Are Truly Greener than Fossil Fuels," FoxNews.com, November 21, 2010. www.foxnews.com.

34. Quoted in Chelsea Anne Young, "Biofuels Boom Could Fuel Rainforest Destruction," *Stanford Report*, February 17, 2009. http://news .stanford.edu.

35. Quoted in Union of Concerned Scientists, "Scientists Warn European Commission over Biofuels Policy," October 7, 2011. www.ucs usa.org.

36. Quoted in Martin LaMonica, "Figuring Land Use into Renewable Energy Equation," CNet.com, May 29, 2010. http://news.cnet .com.

37. Quoted in Erica Gies, "As Ethanol Booms, Critics Warn of Environmental Effect," *New York Times*, June 24, 2010. www.nytimes.com.

38. Quoted in Ron Way, "University Report Warns Water Consumption for Corn-Ethanol on the Rise," *MinnPost*, April 15, 2009. www.minn post.com.

39. Quoted in Carolyn Lochhead, "Dead Zone in Gulf Linked to Ethanol Production," *San Francisco Chronicle*, July 6, 2010. www.sfgate.com.

40. Quoted in Young, "Biofuels Boom Could Fuel Rainforest Destruction."

Chapter Three: Can Biofuels Ever Replace Fossil Fuels?

41. Quoted in Chaudhry, "Advanced Biofuels."

42. Quoted in Erin Voegele, "Senators Talk Biofuels at ACS Briefing, Senate Committee Hearing," *Biodiesel Magazine*, February 3, 2012. www.biodieselmagazine.com.

43. Quoted in Renewable Fuels Association, "Building Bridges to a More Sustainable Future."

44. Quoted in University of British Columbia, "Taking Biofuel from Forest to Highway," February 17, 2012. www.sciencecodex.com.

45. Quoted in Biomass Power Association, "Grand Opening Held for 100-MW Biomass Facility in Florida," *Biomass Power & Thermal*, October 1, 2011. http://biomassmagazine.com.

46. Steven Chu, "Winning the Biofuel Future," US Department of Energy, March 7, 2011. www.whitehouse.gov.

47. Christopher Coons, "Floor Speech: Reforming Ethanol Subsidies and Investing in Advanced Biofuel Development," June 16, 2011. http://coons.senate.gov.

48. Quoted in David Rotman, "The Price of Biofuels," *Technology Review*, January/February 2008. www.technologyreview.com.

49. Quoted in Wenner, "The Next Generation of Biofuels," pp. 46–51.

50. Chevron, "Energy Policy," May 2011. www.chevron.com.

51. Quoted in Matthew L. Wald, "A Bit More Ethanol in the Gas Tank," *New York Times*, October 13, 2010. www.nytimes.com.

52. Rachel Ehrenberg, "The Biofuel Future," *Science News*, August 1, 2009, pp. 24–29.

53. Quoted in Cindy Zimmerman, "EPA Lowers Cellulosic Ethanol Target," Domestic Fuel, December 28, 2011. http://domesticfuel.com.

54. Quoted in Kris Bevill, "Senate Hearing Explores Oil, Energy Outlook," *Ethanol Producer Magazine*, February 3, 2011. http://ethanol producer.com.

55. Quoted in Dan Chapman, "Plant Closure Bursts Ga.'s Biomass Bubble," *Atlanta Journal Constitution*, February 15, 2011. www.ajc .com.

Chapter Four: Should Government Play a Role in Developing Biofuels?

56. Sue Ellerbusch, "Cellulosic Biofuels: A Strategic Option for an Oil Company," BP.com, December 7, 2010. www.bp.com.

57. Quoted in Eric Lipton and Clifford Krauss, "A Gold Rush of Subsidies in Clean Energy Search," *New York Times*, November 11, 2011. www.nytimes.com.

58. Quoted in Lipton and Krauss, "A Gold Rush of Subsidies in Clean Energy Search."

59. Quoted in *Biofuels Digest*, "Government to Invest $510M in Advanced, Drop-In Biofuels," August 16, 2011. www.biofuelsdigest .com.

60. Brent Erickson, "Federal Policy Should Help Capital Flow," *National Journal*, September 27, 2011. http://energy.nationaljournal.com.

61. Quoted in *Biofuels Digest*, "Government to Invest $510M in Advanced, Drop-In Biofuels."

62. Quoted in Environmental News Network, "Sugarcane Ethanol: Brazil's Biofuel Success," January 3, 2008. www.enn.com.

63. Quoted in Science Daily, "Current UK and European Biofuels Policies Are Unethical, Says Report," April 12, 2011. www.sciencedaily .com.

64. Quoted in Conservative Law Foundation, "CLF Statement: New Biomass Energy Regulations for Massachusetts," May 3, 2011. www .clf.org.

65. Quoted in International Energy Agency, "Biofuels Can Provide Up to 27% of World Transportation Fuel by 2050, IEA Report Says," April 20, 2011. www.iea.org.

66. Margo Thorning, "Stop DOE's Double Down on Risky Energy Ventures," *National Journal*, September 29, 2011. http://energy.national journal.com.

67. Nicolas D. Loris, "Government Shouldn't Decide What Cars Should Run On," Heritage Foundation, June 7, 2011. http://blog.heritage .org.

68. Quoted in Gregory DL Morris, "What Is the Real Cost of Cheap Energy?," *Wharton Magazine*, Winter 2012, p. 68.

69. Ben Lieberman and Nicolas D. Loris, "Energy Policy: Let's Not Repeat the Mistakes of the '70s," Heritage Foundation, July 28, 2008. www.heritage.org.

70. Quoted in Debra Saunders, "Solyndra Debacle Spotlights Obama's Folly," *San Francisco Chronicle*, September 4, 2011. www.sfgate.com.

71. Quoted in Saunders, "Solyndra Debacle Spotlights Obama's Folly."

72. William O'Keefe, "Let Markets Shape Our Energy Future," *National Journal*, September 26, 2011. http://energy.nationaljournal.com.

73. Letter to Congress, "Allow the Volumetric Ethanol Excise Tax Credit to Expire," March 1, 2011. www.meatami.com.

74. Quoted in Charlie Dunmore, "Scrap Biofuel Support to Curb Food Costs: Agencies," Reuters.com, June 10, 2011. www.reuters.com.

75. Quoted in Lynn Grooms, "Coalition Writes Congress to Propose Ending VEETC," Farm Industry News, March 4, 2011. www.farm industrynews.com.

76. O'Keefe, "Let Markets Shape Our Energy Future."

Biofuels Facts

Biofuel Production

- Over 90 percent of the gasoline sold in the United States is blended with ethanol.
- According to the Renewable Fuels Association, US ethanol demand averaged 860,000 barrels per day in 2010.
- At the end of 2011 the United States had 204 ethanol biorefineries located in 29 states.
- According to the Renewable Fuels Association, global production of ethanol reached 22.9 billion gallons in 2010.
- According to the US Department of Energy, biomass currently supplies about 3 percent of total US energy consumption in the form of electricity, process heat, and transportation fuels.
- The International Energy Agency predicts that biofuels will provide 27 percent of world transport fuel by 2050.
- According to the International Energy Agency, more than 50 countries have biofuel blending mandates or targets.
- At the start of the twentieth century, Henry Ford planned to fuel his Model Ts with ethanol, and early diesel engines were shown to run on peanut oil.
- About 100 different plants can be used to produce biofuels.

Biofuel Economics

- A car driving on a gallon of ethanol will go only 67 percent as far as a car on a gallon of gasoline.
- Corn feedstock is more expensive to grow than sugarcane per gallon of ethanol produced.
- Between 2001 and 2008 the thermal energy required for ethanol production dropped 28 percent per gallon and electricity per gallon dropped 32 percent, according to the US Department of Agriculture.

- According to the Natural Resources Defense Council, power plants that burn biomass directly can generate electricity at a cost of 7 to 9 cents per kilowatt-hour.

Advanced Biofuels

- The Department of Energy estimates that biofuel production from algae could yield between 4,000 to 6,000 gallons per acre.
- Cellulose is the fiber contained in leaves, stems, and stalks of plants and trees.
- Microalgae, a potential advanced biofuel feedstock, can potentially produce 100 times more oil per acre than soybeans or any other land-based oil crop, according to the Department of Energy.
- The Department of Energy estimates that algae biofuel currently costs more than $8 per gallon using current production technology.

Biofuels and the Environment

- According to the US Department of Energy, cellulosic ethanol has the potential to reduce greenhouse gas emissions by 86 percent.
- According to the University of Minnesota, devoting all US corn and soybean acreage to ethanol and biodiesel production would offset only 12 percent of gasoline and 6 percent of diesel consumption for transportation fuel.
- The transportation sector currently accounts for over a quarter of all US greenhouse gas emissions.

Related Organizations and Websites

Argonne National Laboratory
9700 S. Cass Ave.
Argonne, IL 60439
phone: (630) 252-5580 • fax: (630) 252-5274
e-mail: media@anl.gov • website: www.anl.gov

Argonne National Laboratory is one of the US Department of Energy's largest research centers. Its annual operating budget of about $530 million supports more than 200 research projects, several of which focus on biofuels. The website provides information and papers about biofuel research and ongoing projects.

BioEnergy Science Center
Oak Ridge National Laboratory
PO Box 2008
Oak Ridge, TN 37831
phone: (865) 576-9553 • e-mail: bradleymk@ornl.gov
website: www.bioenergycenter.org

The BioEnergy Science Center is part of the Department of Energy's Oak Ridge National Laboratory. With a team of leading experts and state-of-the-art facility, the center's goal is to develop alternative fuel solutions that are effective and affordable options to petroleum-based fuels. Its website provides news, facts, and general information about biofuels and the energy they can produce.

The Cato Institute
1000 Massachusetts Ave. NW
Washington, DC 20001
phone: (202) 842-0200 • fax (202) 842-3490
website: www.cato.org

The Cato Institute is a public policy research organization dedicated to the principles of individual liberty, limited government, free markets, and peace. Its scholars and analysts conduct independent, nonpartisan research on a wide range of policy issues, including biofuels and renewable energy. The website provides publications on biofuel issues.

Environmental Protection Agency (EPA)
Ariel Rios Bldg.
1200 Pennsylvania Ave. NW
Washington, DC 20460
phone: (202) 272-0167
website: www.epa.gov

The EPA leads the nation in environmental science, research, and education efforts. The mission of the EPA is to protect human health and the environment. The EPA studies biofuels and their effect on the environment and recommends related US policy. The website provides detailed information about the different types of biofuel and their environmental pros and cons.

National Renewable Energy Laboratory (NREL)
1617 Cole Blvd.
Golden, CO 80401
phone: (303) 275-3000
website: www.nrel.gov

The NREL is the Department of Energy's laboratory for renewable energy research and development. Its website has maps, graphs, charts, and reports about renewable energy, including wind power.

Natural Resources Defense Council (NRDC)
40 W. Twentieth St.
New York, NY 10011
phone: (212) 727-2700 • fax: (212) 727-1773
website: www.nrdc.org

The NRDC is a nonprofit environmental action group in the United States. NRDC's major efforts include curbing global warming and moving America beyond oil. It supports the use of biofuels as an alternative to fossil fuels. Its website provides information on the council's current initiatives and an annual report of their progress.

Renewable Fuels Association (RFA)
One Massachusetts Ave. NW, Suite 820
Washington, DC 20001
phone: (202) 289-3835
website: www.ethanolrfa.org

The RFA promotes policies, regulations, and research and development initiatives that promote increased production and use of fuel ethanol. The website provides studies about biofuels, current legislative actions, and the industry outlook.

Union of Concerned Scientists (UCS)
National Headquarters
Two Brattle Sq.
Cambridge, MA 02138
phone: (617) 547-5552 • fax: (617) 864-9405
website: www.ucsusa.org

The Union of Concerned Scientists is the leading science-based non-profit organization working for a healthy environment and a safer world. The website provides information and papers about biofuels and clean energy.

US Energy Information Administration (EIA)
1000 Independence Ave. SW
Washington, DC 20585
e-mail: infoctr@eia.gov • website: www.eia.gov

The EIA analyzes and distributes energy information to promote sound policies and the public understanding of energy and how it interacts with the economy and the environment. The EIA provides information covering energy production, demand, imports, exports, and prices. It prepares reports on topics of current interest, including biofuels and renewable energy.

For Further Research

Books

Leanne Currie-McGhee, *Biofuels*. San Diego: ReferencePoint, 2010.

Matt Doeden, *Green Energy: Crucial Gains or Economic Strains*. Minneapolis: Twenty-First Century Books, 2010.

Paula Johnson, *Biofuels: Sustainable Energy in the 21st Century*. New York: Rosen, 2010.

Wim Soetaert and Erik Vandamme, *Biofuels*. New York: Wiley, 2009.

John Tabak, *Biofuels*. New York: Facts On File, 2009.

Periodicals

David Biello, "The False Promise of Biofuels," *Scientific American*, August 2011.

Erica Gies, "As Ethanol Booms, Critics Warn of Environmental Effect," *New York Times*, June 24, 2010.

Paul Voosen, "Biofuels Future That U.S. Covets Takes Shape—in Brazil," *New York Times*, June 1, 2011.

Internet Sources

Center for Climate and Energy Solutions, "Biofuels Overview." www
.c2es.org/technology/overview/biofuels.

Vinod Khosla, "What Matters in Biofuels & Where Are We?," Khosla Ventures, January 27, 2011. http://www.khoslaventures.com/presentations
/What_Matters_in_Biofuels_2011.pdf.

National Geographic, "Biofuels: The Original Car Fuel." http://environment.nationalgeographic.com/environment/global-warming/biofuel profile.

Renewable Fuels Association, "Building Bridges to a More Sustainable Future: 2011 Ethanol Industry Outlook." http://ethanolrfa.3cdn.net/1ace47565fabba5d3f_ifm6iskwq.pdf.

Websites

Advanced Biofuels Association. http://advancedbiofuelsassociation.com. The Advanced Biofuels Association is a group of companies representing a wide range of technologies in the advanced biofuel industry and serves as an advocate for public policy that encourages the use of biofuels. The website contains industry news, press releases, and the latest information about advanced biofuels.

BP Biofuels. www.bp.com/productlanding.do?categoryId=9030593&contentId=7055794&nicam=USCSEnergy_LabQ408&nisrc=Google&nigrp=Biofuels&nipkw=General&&niadv=biofuels. This webpage, from BP Alternative Energy, offers information, short videos, articles, and interviews about the biofuel industry and advanced biofuels.

Index

Note: Boldface page numbers indicate illustrations.

MERIDIAN MIDDLE SCHOOL
2195 Brandywyn Lane
Buffalo Grove, IL 60089